Feng Shui:
Seeing Is Believing

FENG SHUI:
Seeing Is Believing

Essential Geomancy for Beginners and Skeptics

by Jampa Ludrup

Foreword by Lama Zopa Rinpoche

WISDOM PUBLICATIONS • BOSTON

Wisdom Publications
199 Elm Street
Somerville, MA 02144 USA
www.wisdompubs.org

Library of Congress Cataloging-in-Publication Data

Jampa Ludrup, 1954–
  [Seeing is believing]
 Feng shui : seeing is believing : essential geomancy for beginners and skeptics / by Jampa Ludrup.
    pages cm
 Revision of the author's Seeing is believing.
 ISBN 1-61429-074-1 (pbk. : alk. paper)
 1. Feng shui. 2. Geomancy. I. Title.
 BF1779.F4J36 2013
 133.3'337—dc23
                                          2012025791

ISBN 978-1-61429-074-2; eBook ISBN 978-1-61429-093-3

16 15 14 13 12
5 4 3 2 1

Cover design by Phil Pascuzzo. Interior design by Gopa&Ted2. Set in Joanna MT Pro 11/15.4.

All photos except those on p. 61 are by Jampa Ludrup. The images on pp. 61, 130, 133, 135, 137, 138, and 140–42 are from Thinkstock. The turtle on p. 77 (and on the tearaway card) and the dragon on p. 79 (and throughout) are by Jampa Ludrup and Olivier Massange. The author photo on p. 153 is by Michel Henri.

This book is dedicated with love, gratitude, humility, and respect
to the incomparable Kyabje Lama Zopa Rinpoche.

Contents

Foreword
by Lama Zopa Rinpoche

THOUGH THE MAIN CAUSES of success and difficulties are good karma and negative karma, there are also external conditions that contribute to success and prosperity as well as to problems. Therefore, it's possible to create positive outer conditions that help bring success and stop problems. You can do this by setting up the correct feng shui inside your house and in your surroundings, particularly in important places where you will be over a long period of time. By considering the basic principles of feng shui, you can cure disturbing environments. All of this will help stop the problems that plague you and cause distress, and will help you to succeed in what you want: harmonious relationships, health, education, prosperity, and long life.

Feng shui is an important way for people to improve their lives and help others.

Preface: Seeing Is Believing

WE ALL SEARCH FOR happiness, and yet it can be so elusive. There is no shortage of problems in our lives and we are often too busy or preoccupied to find lasting solutions for them. In the whirlwind of our daily lives it can appear impossible to find a moment's peace in our minds; it seems that we can only respond to the most pressing demands that are placed on us. Small wonder then that the powerful but subtle energies that influence our lives pass unnoticed.

There are many systems of belief that can help us to make sense of the crazy world in which we find ourselves. All the world's major religious philosophies have a message of love, compassion, kindness, and peace at their heart. All are capable of bringing mental peace and happiness. However, they do not have any direct system of causing good fortune to ripen and preventing bad things from happening.

The Chinese have studied the subtle environmental influences that surround us for thousands of years. Over that time they have developed a highly sophisticated system that deals with these subtle energies in such a way that good fortune is encouraged to ripen and bad fortune is avoided. The good news for us Westerners, whose belief systems seem to have little in common with Chinese culture, is that you do not have to believe in it in order for it to work!

The aim of this book is to help you have more happiness in your life by showing you the simple steps you can take to channel and focus the environmental influences that shape your fortunes. With just a few inexpensive, readily available tools you can transform your luck. Even simply changing the direction in which you sit, eat, and sleep can dramatically change your world.

It works. I urge you to try it and reap the benefits in many areas of your life. I know that many of you are skeptical, and rightly so, but in the end, as they say, "Seeing is Believing."

1

Introduction to Geomancy

THIS BOOK IS ABOUT the art of improving your luck by first choosing an environment that is conducive to good luck and then manipulating that environment so that the good luck manifests. In East Asia, this is known as *feng shui*, but I prefer the term *geomancy*. Many Westerners are skeptical about this sort of thing, but the good news is that geomancy works whether you believe in it or not. It does not rely on superstition. I use formulas that I have found to work in my own home and in the hundreds of consultations that I have done over the years. I will attempt to explain the most crucial aspects in a way that I hope will be most approachable for Westerners.

I first came across geomancy when I was traveling with Lama Zopa Rinpoche, a Tibetan monk who is widely acknowledged as a great meditation master. You can imagine my surprise when I discovered that in those days he was spending most of his free time investigating feng shui books rather than Buddhist texts. I come from a scientific background and appreciate Buddhism for its logical approach. So I told Rinpoche, "I am sorry, but you have to allow me to be skeptical about feng shui." He is well known for his very lengthy explanations, but on this occasion he simply said, "It is just cause and effect."

When I subsequently went back to Australia, I decided to put some of the feng shui principles into practice, just as an experiment; I had no particular belief other than faith in Lama Zopa's judgement. I was living very simply in one room, writing and meditating, so it was very easy to put the "right things in the right places." The results were spectacular. I had no money problems; in fact, I had very generous benefactors. My health was good and everything went well. Then, within a few months, I was offered the best job of my life—English studies tutor to the Spanish reincarnated lama, Lama Osel Rinpoche.

As a practicing Buddhist I am always looking for ways to put into practice what I believe to be the essence of Buddhism—"As much as you can, help others. And if you can't help them, at least don't harm them." So with my own practical experience of the power of geomancy, I started to try to help others to achieve the same results. I was immediately encouraged by the effect it had on people's lives. The power of the techniques was confirmed again and again. What started as a hobby began slowly taking over my life, from consultations in Europe, Africa, India, Southeast Asia, and Australia, to running feng shui courses, and now this book.

HISTORY OF GEOMANCY

Geomancy Around the World

There are many forms of geomancy practiced around the world. In Europe a lot of such knowledge was lost during the Middle Ages, but the monuments to it remain. Structures such as Stonehenge in England have slowly revealed their secrets over recent years. The network of paths of subtle energy called "ley lines" that coincide with some of the most spiritual places on Earth has recently come to the forefront of discussion again.

Ley lines can be detected by gifted practitioners using a pendulum, wooden twigs, or metal rods. The rods are bent at a ninety-degree angle at one end and held loosely in each hand. Then you slowly walk over the land to be investigated. When you cross an energy line or a source of water, the rods seemingly cross by themselves. I had some experience of this in India when we were looking for a good place to drill for water. In Europe it is often assumed that a geomancy consultation will include the detection of these lines. There are various techniques of *geobiology*, as it is known, that can locate them. Some involve machinery that is a lot more complicated than metal rods. In my experience, the most important thing about these lines is to not locate your bed or desk above one of them—indeed, anything where you spend a lot of time. Proximity to these lines is a condition for quite serious illnesses, even cancer. So always avoid them if at all possible. When I am checking the best location for a house on a new piece of land for a client, I always try to avoid having any part of the house on these ley lines. The curious thing is that there is no equivalent practice in Chinese feng shui. They seem to be unaware of ley lines and there is no advice on detecting or dealing with any similar energy. However, I think it is important to check your property to see if there are any.

Nowadays, feng shui has taken hold of the European imagination. I have found a lot of interest in my courses and in consultations in Europe in general. Even 10 Downing Street, the residence of the British Prime Minister, was "feng shuied." The words *feng shui* have now entered the Western vocabulary.

Other parts of the world have similar arts. In Africa it seems that *geomancy* means "divination using earth or stones to foretell the future." In Indonesia, I heard of Muslim texts that deal with geomancy techniques. In India there is an advanced form of geomancy called *vaastu*, which is very similar in many ways to the feng shui that is practiced in China. There is some debate about where the practice originated. Some say that vaastu was the precursor of feng shui in China, that it flourished with Buddhism in India and then went through Tibet to China. This seems unlikely as there are ancient Chinese feng shui texts that predate Buddhism. Also, I have not heard of feng shui texts in the Tibetan Buddhist tradition—although it appears the Tibetan non-Buddhist "Black Hat" sect have them. In addition, feng shui is very clearly related to the I Ching, which originated in China about four thousand years ago and was probably practiced in some form even before this. So it seems more likely that vaastu is a derivative of feng shui. Vaastu is widely practiced in India, and is becoming more popular. In general, I have found the feng shui techniques that I will explain here to be more powerful than the vaastu or Tibetan Black Hat systems of geomancy.

These days in China the authorities have repressed the practice of feng shui, and so it is practiced primarily in Taiwan, Hong Kong, Malaysia, and Singapore. Feng shui is also practiced in Korea and Japan. In Korea it is called *p'ung suchirisol*. The founder of the Yi dynasty (1392–1910) in Korea moved the capital to Seoul because the site was said by a monk to fulfill all the requirements of p'ung suchirisol.

There are three main branches of feng shui, which I characterize as the Form School, the Compass School, and the Flying Star School. They are mainly complementary but sometimes contradictory. It is these schools that I will be discussing in this book.

History of Feng Shui

Feng shui is by far the most sophisticated form of geomancy in the world today. It has developed over a period of at least four thousand years in China. China has always had many problems due to floods and strong winds and the art of feng shui was originally developed to try to avert disaster from these elements—*feng* means wind and *shui* means water.

In the beginning of its development, it was practiced by people in every village. However, as the power of the technique became more widely known, it became the sole prerogative of the imperial palace and the ruling classes. Presumably this happened because it was so closely linked to the wisdom of the I Ching, which had an enormous impact on the philosophy of government. It was during the Ming (1368–1644) and Qing (1644–1912) dynasties that feng shui reached its peak of sophistication.

The emperors guarded the secrets of feng shui jealously. Emperor Chu, the founder of the Qing dynasty, is said to have gone as far as spreading fake books on the subject so as to confuse and weaken his enemies. This could be one reason why there are contradictory traditions of feng shui these days. The Forbidden City was designed and built upon feng shui guidelines that would promise success for the inhabitants for hundreds of years. In Japan, for similar reasons, people were forbidden to build any residence with the same orientation as the palace of the emperor in Kyoto.

When the communists took over China, feng shui was banned, although it is said that Mao Zedong followed its principles himself. Practitioners of both feng shui and Taoism were persecuted and many fled from China to the free countries in Southeast Asia. It is in Southeast Asia that feng shui is now most widely practiced, especially in Taiwan, which is the main center for feng shui masters.

Feng Shui Practitioners of Note

Around the world there are many geomancy practitioners and writers—I guess I have become yet another one of them!—but there are three masters in general that I would like to mention.

In Singapore, the Buddhist Reverend Hong Choon was a very great master, particularly of the Form School of feng shui. He was widely reputed to be one of the main advisors to the government and so played an important part in the spectacular success of this small island state. He practiced with a purely altruistic motivation that was immensely admirable and never sought particular success for himself or his monastery.

Two figures that were very important for the spread of feng shui in the West are the Malaysian grand master Yap Cheng Hai and his famous interpreter, who is now a master of the art in her own right: Lillian Too. I first met them in the most holy of Buddhist places: Bodhgaya in northeast India, where Siddhartha became the enlightened Buddha and embarked on his mission to free all beings from suffering.

In the past, feng shui secrets were guarded jealously by the masters and were often only passed on to close disciples when the master was near death. We owe a great debt of gratitude to Yap Cheng Hai for the selfless way in which he has shared his knowledge with so many. Lillian Too, in her turn, has popularized Master Yap's knowledge and that of other masters in a series of highly successful books. She has also added to the body of knowledge through her own observation and the rediscovery of ancient formulas. Both Lillian and Master Yap run very successful courses. I fully acknowledge their encouragement and wisdom in the development of my interest in geomancy.

The I Ching

The source of much of the wisdom of feng shui appears to lie in the I Ching, or "Book of Changes," as it is known. I means "truth" and *ching* means "change." The origins of the I Ching itself are rooted in the distant past. Originally it was developed as a means of divination, but later it also evolved into a philosophical work involving all aspects of good governance and life in general. This was mainly due to the efforts of the famous scholar Confucius. At first, the divination itself was done using animal bones or tortoise shells. Later, yarrow stalks were preferred.

In his excellent and comprehensive new translation of this remarkable book, Alfred Huang says, "The ancient sages watched astronomical phenomena in the sky and topographical features on the earth, and studied the relationships among all beings. They realized that in Heaven and Earth there exists a universal principle that everything is in a continuous process of change. Change is absolute and certain; only the principle of change never changes." The main theme of the I Ching is that everything is in a process of continuous change, rising and falling in a progressive evolutionary advancement.

In this way, the I Ching represents the cosmic balance of the universe. The more we are in tune with the universal forces, the more harmonious our lives will be. This balance is symbolized by the famous circle of yin and yang.

The characteristic called *yang* is applied to the masculine, strong, firm, and active things; *yin* is applied to the feminine, yielding, weak, and passive things. In the symbol, yang is represented by white and yin by black. Yin should not be thought of as negative and undesirable, and yang positive; the yin/yang symbol shows very clearly that yin and yang must embrace each other. It also shows that in the yang it is necessary to have a little yin and in the yin a little yang. This is the way to preserve a proper balance, according to the wisdom of the I Ching.

Confucius

Almost two thousand years after the origins of the I Ching, the famous sage Confucius (551–479 B.C.E.) brought it to a new level of sophistication. He added commentaries called the Ten Wings to the explanations of the trigrams. These commentaries are crucial; without them, divination is very difficult.

Alfred Huang says, "After Confucius and his students had written the commentaries, it became known as a book of ancient wisdom. It is a book that not only tells one who consults it about the present situation and future potential but also gives instruction about what to do and what not to do to obtain good fortune and to avoid misfortune. But one still retains free choice. The guidance is based on comprehensive observations of natural laws by ancient sages and their profound experiences of the laws of cause and effect." The work of Confucius was carried on after his death and the I Ching became more and more refined. By the Song period (960–1279) it was the main philosophical text. It was also the primary source of wisdom on statecraft and was extremely important for the ruling elite of China.

There are many aspects of feng shui that rely on the wisdom of the I Ching; its development was very much bound up with the development of this classic text. As the I Ching developed and became more profound, so did the art of feng shui, until both were at the heart of good governance in imperial China.

BUDDHISM AND FENG SHUI

Over the years I have taken an interest in the links between Tibetan Buddhism and feng shui, and so far I have found that they are very tenuous indeed. Feng shui has been practiced in various forms for at least the last four thousand years.

It therefore predates Buddhism by fifteen hundred years. The link between the cultures of India and China seems to have been through Tibet, and here it seems that the practice of Tibetan astrology holds some clues.

Tibetan culture was far more influenced by India than China, although nowadays it must seem somewhat unique. However, it is very clear that Buddhism is at the very heart of Tibetan culture, and Buddhism came from India. As far as I can ascertain, until quite recently feng shui was practiced in the capital city, Lhasa, but only among the elite families. There is no evidence that it was used in the monasteries at all, and these formed the basis of education in Tibet for centuries. There are some texts that give advice on the orientation and dimensions of temples, but this does not conform to any particular school of feng shui. It may be that the essentially nomadic nature of life in Tibet made the practice of feng shui unnecessary.

In the sixth century C.E. the king of Tibet sent four scholars to China to learn elemental astrology and astronomy. It seems that at this time the Tibetans also absorbed knowledge of these sciences from the Indians, the Arabs, and even the Greeks. The next king, Songtsen Gampo, was responsible for creating a Tibetan written language based on Sanskrit script. He also married a Chinese princess called Wencheng who brought many scholars of classical astrology, astronomy, and medicine with her from China. So at this time, knowledge of the I Ching and feng shui must have been available in Tibet.

Buddhism came to Tibet from India in the eighth century C.E. and quickly flourished. In particular Tantric Buddhism seized the imagination of the Tibetan people; the Tibetans say that in 1027 C.E. the system of meditation known as the Kalachakra Tantra was translated into Tibetan and the practice became widely established. The Kalachakra Tantra clearly describes the cycle of the elements. At death the elements of the body are described as absorbing into each other. Earth dissolves into water, water into fire, fire into air, and air into space. This reflects the destructive cycle of the elements in feng shui. In the Chinese system, air is replaced by metal, and space by wood. The trigrams of the I Ching are also to be found in the iconography of the Kalachakra system.

This rather tenuous link is the closest I can find between geomancy and Buddhism. Maybe more will emerge later. We should not be too surprised at the lack of common ground however. The main focus of geomancy is the manipulation of those outer environmental energies that can cause good fortune to ripen. Buddhism is concerned with the inner mental energies that determine our destiny; it is the internal search for truth and peace that is the driving force in Buddhism, and the outer environment, or destiny, is simply a reflection of our progress in controlling and channelling our inner forces. Put simply, if we always create the right causes, we must always achieve the right effects.

Buddhist monks are sometimes criticized for their interest in feng shui. For one thing, it appears to be mostly derived from Taoist beliefs and not from the words of the Buddha. Additionally, people who practice it are generally looking for some material benefit, which would seem at odds with the more noble aims of a religious philosophy. I can offer no better explanation than Reverend Hong Choon, who told a student that, as a Buddhist, he had a duty to help others. He said it would be wrong for him to watch passively as others strayed from the correct path and not to guide them back.

In my own view, life is hard enough without making it more difficult unnecessarily. How can we hope to find enough peace and space in our minds for loftier and spiritually nourishing pursuits when we are beset by basic problems? Geomancy has some of the answers to these basic problems and so we do indeed have a duty to help others by using its techniques. It is clearly wrong, however, for so-called religious people to use it purely for material gain.

FENG SHUI AND SUPERSTITION

Some people would say that all feng shui is superstition and therefore not worthy of study. Indeed, many writers on the subject include a lot of Chinese superstition in their advice. This involves keeping such objects as three-toed wooden frogs with coins in their mouths, tortoises with dragon's heads, good luck gods, golden sailing ships, strings of Chinese coins, and so on. I am not saying that these things do not work. Maybe they do for some people. Indeed, I met an Englishman in Singapore who always carries a three-toed frog with him for wealth luck. He described a disaster he had at home when his young son accidentally broke the frog. It seems he was in something of a panic to find another one in England before he set off on an important business trip. Curiously though, he seemed rather indifferent to feng shui techniques.

Clearly, we can become rather obsessive about superstitious things in a way that becomes unhealthy. It is important to keep a sensible balance in one's life and not to worry unnecessarily. I do not recommend that my Western clients buy a lot of Chinese objects; they generally do not fit with the overall décor and style of the house and there is no point in trading a set of Western superstitions for Chinese ones.

However, it is clear to me that feng shui itself can be practiced in a non-superstitious way. That has been my approach, and the recommendations I make are generally the essential ones that I have found to work whether you believe them or not. If you want to follow Chinese superstition that is up to you, but in my experience it is not necessary for successful feng shui practice.

Can Geomancy Really Make Us Happy?

This is a difficult question to answer. So much depends on the individual and their way of thinking. I have done consultations for many materially rich people with some magnificent houses. Paradoxically, these have also been some of the most unhappy people, with the most worrying problems. We all seem to regard material progress as the yardstick of success in our society. We have an insatiable desire for bigger houses in better neighborhoods, luxury cars, labor-saving devices, and better entertainment. We are constantly looking for better paying, more interesting occupations. Sometimes this is driven by the desire to provide the very best for our children. Sometimes it is simply the desire for higher status. We subconsciously believe that these acquisitions will help us to be happy. Ironically, it seems that possessions end up owning us. Maintaining a luxurious lifestyle can become a burden in itself.

People turn to geomancy hoping that there is an easier way to create good fortune. Indeed, there is nothing intrinsically wrong with the wish to find happiness. It is innate in every living being. But to think that it solely comes from material possessions is wrong. There is nothing intrinsically wrong with having material possessions either, but if they come at the expense of a good heart then they can bring you no benefit in the long run.

The very worst that can happen with geomancy is that it becomes your new unhealthy obsession. We Westerners are always hoping for quick and easy solutions to problems. We turn to religion, astrology, numerology, palmistry, yoga, exercise, new-age therapies, meditation, and geomancy, hoping to make sense of our crazy world. Some people flit from one to another looking for a quick fix. However, all of them require some perseverance in order to find benefit.

Meditation and geomancy have one thing in common. When you start meditation and look at your mind all you can see is clutter, disarray, and things hopelessly out of place. Similarly, when you first look at the geomancy of your house, all you can see are faults—the door is facing the wrong way; the bed has to be put in the corner; the right-hand building is higher than the left; there is no water in front. It can drive you crazy!

No house is perfect and it is very rare for a house to be a complete disaster either. The trick is to make the best of what you have; to make it work for you as best you can. Every house can be improved—and believe me, if you are living in a house that has really bad geomancy for you, you know it already. Just try to apply the geomancy techniques and then forget about it for a couple of months. Then check if there has been any benefit. Constantly worrying about whether you have done it right and whether it will work or not will not help you.

My first Buddhist teacher, Venerable Geshe Dawo, used to tell me, "Worry doesn't help. If there is something you can do, you do it and there is no need to worry. If there is nothing you can do, why worry?" Geomancy can help you to take control of the external environmental forces that shape your life, but if you want to be really, truly happy you must take control of your mind and your heart.

Anyway, enough of the theory of geomancy and how it came into being—you want to know what advice it can give you and how to put it into practice. I will try to explain, in the most logical order I can, what you most need to know in order to have more success in your life.

FUNDAMENTALS OF GEOMANCY

Looking for Luck

People use geomancy to try to improve their luck, but luck is a relative thing. If you have enjoyed a rich lifestyle since you were young, you may feel unlucky if you suddenly have to go without something you consider essential, like a car. However, someone living in the slums in India may consider you to be very lucky indeed, even without a car. On the other hand you may find that many people in India are luckier spiritually than you are. It depends on your priorities and circumstances, and these change as we age and go through life. But whatever kind of luck you are hoping for, where does it come from and how does it manifest? And why is it that geomancy seems to work for some but not for others?

There is an old saying in business circles that there is "No such thing as a free lunch." The same thing applies to geomancy. Luck is not just spirited out of nowhere. In order to have a beneficial result, there must first be a positive action—in order to receive good fortune, you must first do good. That positive action creates a seed, which will ripen into a positive result when the right conditions come together. Then it is up to you to seize the opportunity that appears. Geomancy provides the cooperative conditions through which the good luck becomes manifest. This is what Lama Zopa meant when he said, "It is just cause and effect."

In this way geomancy makes up only one third of your luck. The first third is creating the causal seed through a positive action, the second third is making the seed ripen through geomancy, and the last third is recognising and seizing the opportunity that is created. In the same way, negative actions create seeds for negative results, and bad environmental energy will allow those seeds to ripen, and then you will experience bad luck. This is where geomancy is so critical for the type of luck we experience in life, and why some houses and businesses are luckier than others for us.

The dominant philosophy in the West is scientific materialism. We demand logical and empirical explanations for everything and cannot accept the existence of subtle physical and mental forces. We think of ourselves as individuals, responsible for our own lives; more and more we are disconnected from our fellow beings and our environment. We cannot see any connection between how we live our lives and the fortune we experience. More than that, we cannot see the basic inter-connectedness of all things. We actually depend upon one another and our environment for survival, yet somehow we believe we depend ultimately only on ourselves. We say "I make my own luck," and to some extent that is true, but that luck is made in dependence on others and ripens in dependence on our environment—good reasons to cherish both!

Creating Luck

To create good luck you must first have a good intention. The more pure the intention, the better the result. So for instance if you give money to a beggar in the hope that it will improve his life, that is a better motivation than giving it to him to get rid of your loose change. Both actions are positive, but the former is made much more so by the intention. The more unselfish the motivation, the better.

Each type of luck—whether wealth, health, relationship luck, or help from mentors—has its cause. For instance, generosity is the cause of wealth. My mother used to ruefully say, "Much gets more." In our family we never had much opportunity to be generous with money. But one can also be generous of spirit, giving what little you can to those who give you the opportunity. You can be generous just with your time, your love, and your support. The more giving you are, the more seeds of wealth are created. The more noble the intention, the more seeds are created. As they ripen, you can create a flow of wealth that can benefit many and, by the way, create more seeds of wealth. In that way "much" does indeed "get more."

From a Buddhist point of view, we have all had many previous lifetimes, during which we may have taken the opportunity to create positive seeds. Such seeds are carried forward with us from life to life. This is why the most miserly person still has the possibility of his or her wealth luck ripening, and why people who act in a negative way in general may still appear to have good luck—they still have positive luck from their previous lives. The problem for them is that they are exhausting their stores of seeds and they will run out one day.

Of course, this is a Buddhist perspective and you can accept it or leave it as you see fit. The point is that geomancy works regardless of your philosophical beliefs, so you can reap the benefits whether you are religious, atheist, or agnostic.

Making Luck Manifest

There are two ways to make good luck manifest. You can pray to a higher power, or you can manipulate your environment in a positive way. Sometimes the former will lead you automatically to the latter. For those who do not believe in higher powers, then geomancy is essential.

People are often afraid that when they invite the geomancer they risk being told to break walls and move swimming pools. In fact it is rarely so drastic. Usually improvements can be made by placing a small water feature such as a fish tank, hanging a couple of wind chimes, moving some pots and flowers, and putting a lamp here and there. Often it is simply a matter of relocating things that you already own. In this way, it is very affordable and certainly need not be very expensive.

How do we assess whether geomancy has affected our luck or not? We have some idea of our general circumstances and whether they are steadily improving or not. Sometimes we feel there is some unexplained obstacle that prevents us from achieving something that we expect. When you use geomancy, the block is removed or there is some other unexpected beneficial result. Sometimes the result is quite subtle or can come in a disguised way, so you do not always spot the potential benefit immediately. You may even miss it entirely due to some predisposition or habit that makes you keep looking elsewhere for opportunity. Often however, the change is unmistakable. Some water features can bring unexpected wealth within as little as nine days. Normally you would expect a result within a few months.

Seizing Luck

When the opportunity presents itself, you must seize good luck and make it work for you. All kinds of opportunities may come, but if you are lazy or inattentive they will just pass you by. Quite often opportunities come but we fail to recognize them because we are so set in our ways that we think that they lie outside of our expertise or ability. We can only take full advantage if we are prepared to look "outside of the box." We must be prepared to go beyond our normal mindset.

For example, a friend of mine in Kuala Lumpur had his heart set on working in interior design and was completely absorbed in redesigning his family home in order to launch his career. His house should have been very lucky, but I detected a blockage in the orientation of the front door. Removing the metal security grille was enough; within two days he had a wonderful and unexpected offer that set him off on a completely different and successful career.

There are many other factors that affect our ability to take full advantage of our good luck: our physical health, self-confidence, emotional stability, and general level of education. If we improve these factors it seems that our "luck" improves. In fact, we are simply better able to seize the opportunities when they come.

Dealing with "Bad" Luck

In geomancy we are usually obsessed with the creation of "good" luck. But sometimes "bad" luck is not necessarily a negative thing. Often, it is adversity that helps us grow. I became interested in Buddhism and subsequently in geomancy after an illness that lasted three months. I had been overdoing it in the corporate world and now had to pay for it. During my illness, I had to rest completely, and after exhausting my interest in the local video library I picked up a book by the Dalai Lama in the New Age bookshop next door. This opportunity completely transformed my life in a most beneficial way. I went from computers to compassion. I can truly say that the illness was one of the best things that ever happened to me.

They say, "Every cloud has a silver lining." It is important not to become too obsessed with geomancy, otherwise you may blame every little negative thing that happens to you on your environment and you may miss the "silver lining" that is there in all of life's problems. In any case, geomancy is never perfect. It is impossible to create the perfect house—otherwise there would still be Chinese emperors. Every building has some negative aspects and it impossible to fix all of them with geomancy. We can only try to minimize them.

There are many ways to solve life's problems. Obviously, the solutions that cause the most benefit and the least harm are the best and there are many philosophies and religions that can help you to understand how to achieve them. But your environment also plays a crucial role in both the arising of and the solution to problems. That is what prompted Lama Zopa Rinpoche to say to me, "The best way to help people is with religious philosophy—the next best is geomancy."

Environmental Influences

Environmental influences are a major factor in creating the conditions for your luck to manifest itself. Some are much more obvious than others.

Gross Environmental Influences

It is very clear how our gross physical environment has a major effect on our lives. Noise, weather and climate, industrial pollution, and general geography and geology all influence our general well-being. The presence of a major land feature such as a great mountain or volcano can even induce a more spiritual view of life. We see this in such places as Nepal and Bali. In Bali, the active volcano Mount Agung has a brooding presence that pervades the island. The people practice a very active form of Hinduism and make extensive offerings every day to pacify the local spirits and placate Agung. It seems to work, and most visitors are impressed with the spirituality, peace, and creativity of the people who live there. In Nepal and Tibet the high mountains have had a major effect on the culture of the inhabitants. It seems that such harsh conditions are very conducive to spiritual practice. I have always been amazed at the sunny dispositions and generosity of those who live in such places.

It seems that industrial and other pollution always has a damaging effect on people. The spirits of those who live under such conditions are usually low. Pollution has a depressing effect on a society and people can feel quite hopeless. The more polluted an environment becomes, the less incentive people feel they have to keep it clean. It is a vicious cycle that results in worse conditions.

These days we suffer from other pollution also. We are surrounded by an increasingly pervasive network of electromagnetic radiation. All electronic devices give off this kind of radiation, from electric kettles to mobile phones. The behavior of some animals can be severely affected by it. For instance, some species of bees will attack any electrical object, seeing it as a threat to the community. Fire ants in the southern United States are so strongly attracted to electrical radiation that they will take up residence in traffic lights, computers, and other equipment, causing chaos. Some writers of books on geomancy make mention of electromagnetic radiation as a negative influence. However, I would find it much harder to live without these radiation-causing gadgets and, as far as I know, there is no proven scientific link between low-level radiation and disease, as everyone fears there is. However, it does seem to make sense to reduce your exposure as much as possible and so I agree with those that suggest we should reduce the amount of electrical gadgetry in the bedroom. After all, that is where we spend most of our time. This just seems to be common sense to me, and not geomancy.

Also in the realm of common sense is the effect of the absence or presence of clutter. A cluttered environment is the result of a cluttered or careless mind rather than the cause of it. When you clear it up you are ordering your environment in a positive and comprehensible way and this must have a beneficial effect on the mind—and also on your ability to grasp opportunities when they come.

Wind and water are the major influences on those that live close to nature—indeed, as I mentioned, *feng* means "wind" and *shui* means "water." A strong wind can either provide a lot of energy or can be tiring and unsettling. When I was a schoolteacher we used to dread windy days because the children would be full of a kind of wild energy that was hard for us to handle. The sea has enormous power and just watching it can change our mood. Water gives life and we all appreciate the presence of it, but it can also be destructive. It seems that every year there are more and more floods in different places around the world—a clear sign that we are not taking proper care of our environment.

These gross environmental influences are very obvious. It is very clear where the good and bad locations are from this point of view. So I do not need to explain to you which parts of the world, which countries, and which regions are likely to be "lucky"—usually this is very clear to you because it is where the fortunate people live! However, I can give some reasons why certain places may be luckier than others.

Subtle Environmental Influences

It is not so clear how our environment can affect us in subtle ways, and indeed this has been the subject of careful observation in Asia for thousands of years. These subtle influences exist both inside the building and outside in the immediate vicinity. Some are related to the general topography or landforms around the building; these influences are the subject of study of the Form School of geomancy. Others are related to the best orientation of an individual person within the building; this is the area of expertise of the Compass School. More difficult to understand are the influences of the elements (earth, fire, water, metal, and wood) in various parts of the property. Even more subtly hidden are the periodic influences that depend on the orientation and age of the building itself. This is the field of study of the Flying Star School.

The external influences of the Form School include the presence of hills, large buildings, trees, towers, and transmitters. The location and flow of water is very important, as are the roads that lead to and from the property. The Form School also gives advice for the inside of the building—the positioning of doors, beds, shelving, pillars, and so on.

In the Compass School the emphasis is on the orientation of the building in relation to personal good and bad directions that are based on your year of birth. Similarly, the orientation of your bed, workplace, and doors are crucial. In many years of consultation I have found the advice of this school to be the most easy to apply and particularly effective. It also deals with the proper location of the various elements, such as wood and metal, within the building and the surrounding land. It is the Form School and Compass School recommendations that I will mainly be dealing with in this book.

The Flying Star School is the hardest to understand and explain. It requires some skill with a magnetic compass, a good understanding of the Compass School, and strong familiarity with the cycles of elements, which I will explain later. A good understanding of the I Ching is also very useful. Flying Star is the most powerful form of geomancy but its full breadth and depth are beyond the scope of this introductory text, though I will outline those areas of Flying Star that are essential to know at first.

The Chinese call the subtle environmental influences *sheng chi* or "heaven's breath." Negative influences are called *shar chi* or "killing breath." In both cases, when the *chi* energy is encouraged to slow down and meander, it becomes beneficial, and when it travels quickly and in straight lines, it can become detrimental to good fortune.

It is difficult to offer a hypothesis for the origin and nature of these environmental forces. Clearly they have something to do with magnetism—both the earth's magnetic field and the influence of various objects upon it. By manipulating these you can definitely change your luck. The forces also clearly have something to do with the gravity exerted by large landforms and by celestial objects. But as of yet, there is no instrument that can entirely measure these subtle influences.

Like astrology, the practice of geomancy varies greatly in the quality of the practitioners. A poor practitioner will give both arts a bad name. Neither practice is yet scientific in the strict sense of the word, although both are based on centuries of careful observation of cause and effect. The recommendations that I will give in this book have been given by many masters over the centuries, and by myself in many consultations, and thus my recommendations have the weight of both history and personal experience. I urge you to try them for yourself and then you will see the results.

The Trigrams

Now let us turn our attention to the trigrams of the I Ching. During the Xia dynasty (2005–1766 B.C.E.), the eight trigrams, or *gua*, were invented by the sage Fu Xi. The trigrams consist of sets of three broken and unbroken lines, representing yin and yang respectively. He assigned characteristics to each one of the eight for the purposes of divination. He then arranged them in an order that is now known as the Early Heaven Ba Gua.

In this arrangement, the most yang trigram, which has three unbroken lines, is at the top and the most yin, with its three broken lines, is opposite it. Similarly, the other six trigrams are paired, facing their opposite. The most yang trigram is called Qian, which is translated as "initiating." The most yin trigram is called Kun, which means "responding." By convention, the top of the Ba Gua represents the southern direction; so in this case Qian is located in the south and Kun in the north. Fu Xi arranged the trigrams in this way to represent the heavenly arrangement of universal forces. This is most useful for divination and in the location and orientation of burial sites.

The next important figures in the development of the I Ching were King Wen and his son, the Duke of Zhou. They lived in the twelfth century B.C.E. and were responsible for a major development in the use of the trigrams of Fu Xi. King Wen devised the arrangement of one trigram on top of another. The result is a hexagram composed of six yin and yang lines. There are sixty-four possible combinations. King Wen ascribed meanings to each of the sixty-four hexagrams, called Decisions. The Duke of Zhou was responsible for then giving interpretations of each of the individual lines in the hexagram. Alfred Huang explains that, "The arrangement of the hexagrams is in a connected, rising and falling sequence of cyclic change."

King Wen was also responsible for a new arrangement of the trigrams of the Ba Gua. Here, the trigram Li—"Brightness"—is placed at the top, or south, and *Kan*—"Darkness"—is opposite. This arrangement reflects the "earthly" nature of change; it is concerned with humans and their activities in relation to the heavenly forces. This is called the Later Heaven Ba Gua and is used in the dwellings of the living. It is this type of geomancy that I will explain in this book.

In this arrangement Qian is located in the northwest and Kun in the southwest. This is very important in Compass School geomancy, as we will see later.

Characteristics of the Trigrams

As feng shui developed, more characteristics were added to the trigrams, in addition to the original ones described by Fu Xi. For instance, a color, element, shape, and family member were assigned to each trigram, and hence to each direction, as summarized in the table below. This became crucial in the practice of Compass School geomancy.

Trigram				
Name	Li	Kun	Dui	Qian
Direction	S	SW	W	NW
Number	9	2	7	6
Character	Brightness	Responding	Joyful	Initiating
Feature	Fire	Earth	Lake	Heaven
Season	Summer	Between	Autumn	Autumn
Element	Fire	Big earth	Small metal	Big metal
Family member	Middle daughter	Mother	Youngest daughter	Father
Color	Red	Ocher	White/Metallic	White/Metallic
Shape	Triangular	Square	Round	Round
Animal	Phoenix	Cow	Tiger	Horse
Luck	Reputation	Relationships	Children	Mentors
Body feature	Eyes	Stomach/Womb	Mouth/Speech	Head/Mind/Lungs

Trigram				
Name	Kan	Gen	Zhen	Xun
Direction	N	NE	E	SE
Number	1	8	3	4
Character	Darkness	Keeping still	Taking action	Proceeding humbly
Feature	Water	Mountain	Thunder	Wind
Season	Winter	Between	Spring	Spring
Element	Water	Small earth	Big wood	Small wood
Family member	Middle son	Youngest son	Eldest son	Eldest daughter
Color	Blue/Black	Ocher	Green	Light green
Shape	Wavy	Square	Rectangle	Rectangle
Animal	Turtle	Elephant	Dragon	Rooster
Luck	Career	Knowledge	Health	Wealth
Body feature	Ears	Hands/Fingers	Legs/Feet	Hips/Thighs

The Lo Shu Magic Square

Another fundamental of feng shui is the Lo Shu square. According to legend, a tortoise was found on the banks of the Lo River that had a strange pattern of dots that represented numbers etched on its back. Either this pattern corresponded exactly with the trigrams of the Later Heaven Ba Gua, or King Wen used it for inspiration in devising the Later Heaven arrangement. However it came into being, the Lo Shu square is the fundamental basis of both Compass School and Flying Star School geomancy.

The remarkable thing about the Lo Shu square is that the numbers add up to fifteen in any direction—horizontally, vertically, or diagonally. If you check the Later Heaven Ba Gua arrangement and replace the trigrams with their corresponding numbers (as shown in the table above) you find that they are exactly the same as in the Lo Shu square. Note that the number five is included to represent the center of the Ba Gua and south is at the top. So the Lo Shu square gives a simple way to show the relationship of the numbers of the Later Heaven Ba Gua.

As you can see from the table of the trigrams, each one has an element associated with it. It was found that a grid of the Lo Shu square could be applied to the layout of a building and it became very important for determining the exact placement of each element for each of its nine areas. I will explain the application of the Lo Shu square to a property in later chapters.

The Relationships of the Elements

The original text of the I Ching did not mention the importance of the five elements. It was during the Han dynasty (206 B.C.E. to 220 C.E.) that the elements—earth, fire, water, wood, and metal—were integrated with the trigrams. This then became an integral part of the I Ching and feng shui as well as Chinese astrology. Understanding the trigrams and the relationship of the elements associated with them is extremely important in geomancy.

The relationships are explained in four cycles of the elements: productive, exhaustive, destructive, and supportive. They are also known respectively as the mother, son, enemy, and friend cycles. In order to practice geomancy effectively it is essential that you understand these cycles well. Placing the right elements in the right places within the building and its grounds can make good luck ripen. If you have the wrong elements there, then bad luck may ripen instead!

The Productive Cycle

In the productive (or mother) cycle, fire produces earth, earth produces metal, metal produces water, water produces wood, and wood produces fire. To help you remember this cycle you can think of it in the following way: When fire burns, earth or ash is produced. Earth produces metal through mining and chemical extraction. Metal produces water in the way a metal tap does, or a metal bowl or cup holds water. Water produces wood because rain is needed for trees and plants to grow. And wood produces fire when it is ignited.

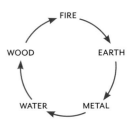

The productive cycle is used to enhance the luck of any particular sector of the building under consideration. This will be explained in detail later.

The Destructive Cycle

In the destructive (or enemy) cycle, fire destroys metal, metal destroys wood, wood destroys earth, earth destroys water, and water destroys fire. That is to say—fire melts metal, metal cuts wood, the roots of trees and plants displace and consume the earth, earth soaks up water, and water puts out fire.

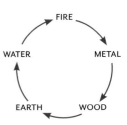

The Exhaustive Cycle

The exhaustive (or son) cycle is the reverse of the productive (mother) cycle. It seems that sons tend to exhaust their mothers! So, fire exhausts wood, wood exhausts water, water exhausts metal, metal exhausts earth, and earth exhausts fire. In other words—fire burns up and exhausts the supply of wood, trees and

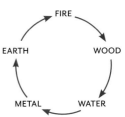

plants suck up water, water rusts metal, metal machines dig up the earth and exhaust its resources, and earth can be put on a fire to extinguish it.

The exhaustive cycle is used in geomancy to control negative influences involving the other elements. This is mainly used in Flying Star geomancy.

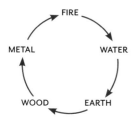

The Supportive Cycle

The supportive (or friend) cycle is the reverse of the destructive cycle. In this cycle of the elements, fire supports water, water supports earth, earth supports wood, wood supports metal, and metal supports fire. In other words, if you use fire to heat water you get steam energy and power; if you water the earth, plants can grow; wooden handles help us to use metal implements; and metal tools can be used to control fire and make it useful. However, it is important to use the elements sparingly in this cycle. For example, too much water on the earth creates mud, and applying too much fire to water will boil it all away.

This cycle is used more in Chinese and Tibetan astrology, but it is also important in element analysis in geomancy.

The table of the trigrams shows the ideal element for each location, but I will explain the use of the elements and their cycles in much more detail when we start to look at Compass School geomancy.

2

Personal Geomancy

I N THE HUNDREDS of consultations that I have done over the years, I have found that the single most important thing for people to know is their "good" and "bad" directions. This is the first thing I check when I start the reading for a house or business. Everybody has auspicious and inauspicious directions, which are based on the year of birth. There is a simple formula that can be used to work out your trigram number, or gua number, as it is known. From this you find out which directions suit you. The formula for personal directions comes from a Compass School text that was discovered by Grand Master Yap Cheng Hai.

It seems that we have an internal subtle energy that becomes aligned with the external subtle environmental energy at the time of birth. In Buddhism, great meditators are able to control this internal subtle energy in a most profound way. In general, people fall into one of two groups. You are either "East" group or "West" group. If you are in the East group, then north, south, east, and southeast are good directions for you. If you are in the West group then west, southwest, northwest, and northeast are good.

First of all, you must have a good quality magnetic compass and be able to read it accurately. This is more difficult than it sounds for some people. Compasses vary greatly in quality and price. A cheap one is rarely of any use because the needle is usually only weakly magnetic and is easily deflected as you move around. They often stick in a misleading position. The best ones are made for orienteering and trekking. European compasses such as the Silva brand are good quality and can be found in good outdoor-gear stores. Get the staff to show you how to use it properly if you are not sure. A strongly magnetic compass needle will hold its direction as you swivel the compass case around; this shows that it is good quality. You can keep a small compass of lesser quality for a quick check of directions when you are out and about. Smart phone compass applications are not usually very reliable.

When you start to experiment with your compass, the first thing you will notice is the incredible variation that can be observed inside a building. There is probably nothing wrong with the compass; if there is a large amount of metal used in the construction of a building, it can drive a compass wild. This is particularly true of modern apartment blocks. In the kitchen of one flat in Malaysia, where I did a reading, it did not matter which way you faced: every direction was north! This was due to a very large pillar in the center of the room that must have been very heavily reinforced with metal. In such places, geomancy becomes very difficult.

In another place I noticed a very strange difference in the direction of the left-hand side of the bed in the master bedroom where the wife slept, to the right-hand side of the bed where the husband slept. The left was north and the right was northeast. When I walked behind into the dressing room the puzzle was solved. There was a large metal safe behind the head of the bed!

DETERMINING YOUR GUA NUMBER

Once you have your compass, you must work out your gua number. This is based on the Chinese lunar calendar, which starts in January or February of each year. To work out your gua number you can use the following formula:

Please note that you must be careful when calculating your gua number if you were born in January or February, as the Chinese New Year can fall anywhere between January 21 and February 19. So if you were born before January 21 then you must use the previous year for the calculation. For example, if you were born on January 15, 1985, you must use 1984 in the calculation.

Birth Dates up to 1999

Males

- ► Take the last two digits of the year of birth
- ► Add them together, and if the resulting sum is two digits, add those digits together to reduce them to a single number
- ► Deduct from ten

For example, if you were born in 1954:
- ► Add the last two digits together: 5 + 4 = 9
- ► Deduct the sum from ten: 10 − 9 = 1

Your gua number is one.

Females

- ► Take the last two digits of the year of birth
- ► Add them together, and if the resulting sum is two digits, add those digits together to reduce them to a single number
- ► Add five and, if necessary, reduce the sum to a single number again

For example, if you were born in 1979:
- ► Add the last two digits together: 7 + 9 = 16
- ► Reduce the sum to one number: 1 + 6 = 7
- ► Add five: 7 + 5 = 12
- ► Reduce the sum to one number: 1 + 2 = 3

Your gua number is three.

Birth Dates after 2000

Males

- ► Take all the digits of the year of birth
- ► Add them together and reduce them to a single number
- ► Deduct from eleven

For example, for those born in 2001:
- ► Add all the digits together: 2 + 0 + 0 + 1 = 3
- ► Deduct the sum from eleven: 11 − 3 = 8

Your gua number is eight.

Females

- ► Take all the digits of the year of birth
- ► Add them together and reduce them to a single number
- ► Add four and, if necessary, reduce the sum to a single number again

For example, for those born in 2008:
- ► Add all the digits together: 2 + 0 + 0 + 8 = 10
- ► Reduce to a single number: 1 + 0 = 1
- ► Add four: 1 + 4 = 5

Your gua number is five.

If you were born between January 21 and February 19, you must check the table in the appendix to find your gua number. If you are not sure, check the table anyway. I feel it is important to be precise about this as I have seen big changes in fortune around the Chinese New Year and if you turn out to be West group rather than East group, or vice versa, it can make a huge difference.

Personal Directions

Your gua number determines whether you are in the East or West group, and which directions are lucky and unlucky for you. Some people say that these directions should be reversed in the southern hemisphere, that your lucky directions there should be opposite to the recommendations of the Chinese, who are located in the northern hemisphere. This is not true. They are based on compass directions. North is north, and south is south, whether you are in Australia or Norway.

As you can see from the following tables, everyone has four good directions (the first four rows) and four bad directions (the last four rows). It is up to you to determine which direction you consider to be the most important of the good directions. Most people choose wealth and this is often called the "best direction."

East Group Directions

Direction Gua no.	1	3	4	9
Wealth	SE	S	N	E
Health	E	N	S	SE
Relationships	S	SE	E	N
Development	N	E	SE	S
Unlucky	W	SW	NW	NE
Five ghosts	NE	NW	SW	W
Six killings	NW	NE	W	SW
Total loss	SW	W	NE	NW

West Group Directions

Direction Gua no.	5 Male	5 Female	2	6	7	8
Wealth	NE	SW	NE	W	NW	SW
Health	W	NW	W	NE	SW	NW
Relationships	NW	W	NW	SW	NE	W
Development	SW	NE	SW	NW	W	NE
Unlucky	E	S	E	SE	N	S
Five ghosts	SE	N	SE	E	S	N
Six killings	S	E	S	N	SE	E
Total loss	N	SE	N	S	E	SE

Good Directions

Wealth This is the best direction for bringing money luck. It is also said to bring a high and honorable position.

Health This is the best direction for health luck. It can cure inexplicable long-term illnesses. You can expect a middling amount of wealth and good friends.

Relationships This direction brings relationship luck. It brings harmonious family relationships. It can stop family problems such as quarrelling between couples, or parents and children. It can help those who are unable to have children or to find a partner.

Development This direction is associated with growth and personal development. It is important for education and spiritual growth. All children should use this direction until they are fully-grown. It brings a good life without spectacular wealth. I am using this direction as I write this book.

Bad Directions

Unlucky This direction brings accidents and mishaps. There are problems but they are not extreme.

Five Ghosts With this direction you could suffer from fire and burglary. If you are a businessperson your employees may leave you. Your youngest child could get hurt. There are quarrels and a lack of peace at home and work.

Six Killings This direction causes grievous harm to the family and business. There are legal problems, illness, and even death.

Total Loss This direction is as bad as its name implies and should be avoided at all costs. The family may split or there could be ill health or even death. You may lose all your descendants and the family name may come to an end. You could lose all your wealth. You will feel that everything is going wrong.

Now that you understand the benefits of using the good directions and the drawbacks of the bad directions, you need to know how to use the good ones and avoid the bad ones. As much as possible, your house, office, bedroom, desk and bed should be aligned with your good directions. This is sometimes very difficult to achieve. The most important aspects to look at are the direction of your front door and the orientation of your bed.

DOOR DIRECTION

I was once invited to do a reading on a home by the daughter of the family. As usual, I started by asking her for the birth dates of all the family members and I calculated everyone's gua numbers. Next I checked the direction of the front door. I was surprised to see that it was oriented in her father's "Total Loss" direction. "How long has your family been living here?" I asked. "Ten years," she replied. "Then you have got your father's year of birth wrong," I said. She looked very surprised but rang him up and, sure enough, he was actually born in the previous year. That made him West group rather than East group and made the front door direction beneficial for him and the whole family.

The point of this story is to show you how crucial a good front door direction is. There is no way that the head of the family can live contentedly for ten years with a front door that faces the Total Loss direction. He or she would feel so uncomfortable in the house and there would be so many mishaps that the family would want to move after a relatively short time. Most people would intuitively sense that the house was not going to be any good for them when they first saw it. If the main door direction suits the head of the family then the good luck flows on to the whole family.

How do you check the door direction? Most masters recommend taking three readings. The first should be taken in the doorway itself with the compass at waist height. The reading is always taken from the inside looking out. Take three paces straight backward and take another reading. Take another three paces back and take the third reading. You will probably notice some variation in the direction of the three readings, but hopefully it is not too major. If there is a variation of 45 degrees or more, it means that there is a lot of metal in the construction of your building and it will be difficult to apply geomancy techniques reliably.

Use the following table to check the directions accurately.

The front door is the mouth of the house and is absolutely crucial. It is where heaven's breath (the beneficial energy) enters and it must come from a beneficial direction for you. If you are in doubt about the three readings, I believe the most important is the one taken in the doorway itself. Sometimes, rather annoyingly, the compass reading appears to be right in the line between two directions. For instance, if the reading is 337.5 degrees, is the direction north or northwest? I have found that when this happens the energy is blocked. However, it is easily fixed by placing a large metal object next to the door so that the compass reading is deflected into the most beneficial direction. You need to experiment a little to get it right.

Direction	Compass reading
South	158 to 202 degrees
Southwest	203 to 247 degrees
West	248 to 292 degrees
Northwest	293 to 337 degrees
North	338 to 22 degrees
Northeast	23 to 67 degrees
East	68 to 112 degrees
Southeast	113 to 157 degrees

Sitting and Facing Directions of the Building

If your gua number is one, making you part of the east group, your wealth direction is southeast and you would think that a front door facing that way is best for you. However we must take into account both the "facing" direction of the house and its "sitting" direction. The facing direction is the direction the front door faces. The sitting direction is the direction the back of the house faces. So a house that faces southeast sits northwest (the opposite direction).

As northwest is the Six Killings direction for gua one, then that is no good. Likewise if your gua number is six, putting you with the west group, your best direction is west. But a house that faces west is sitting east, which is the Five Ghosts direction, so that also is no good.

So the only really good front door orientations for those in the east group are north or south, and for those in the west group they are northeast or southwest. This means that people with gua numbers one, nine, six, and seven should not use the wealth direction for their front door. Those with gua one or nine should live in houses with front doors that face north or south and those with gua six or seven should have houses that face northeast or southwest.

Apartments

In apartment buildings you have two doors to check—the door into the building on the ground floor and the door into your apartment. Hopefully, both are good directions for you. Indeed, ideally, the two doors face the same direction. If one of the doors faces the Unlucky direction it is manageable. But if one of them faces the Five Ghosts, Six Killings, or Total Loss direction, then you will most likely experience some very bad luck. However, you still have two important directions to check inside your house or apartment: your bed direction and the direction you usually sit facing.

Businesses

Businesses are similar to apartments in that there is often more than one front door. Try to have as many doors as possible in your good directions. Then there is the orientation of your own workspace or office. As you are probably there for most of the day, it is important to be facing your good directions as much as possible. Your luck at work is also influenced strongly by the geomancy of your home. Do not expect much good fortune in your business if you have not sorted out your house first.

Bedroom

You must now check the direction of your bedroom door. Again, you take the compass reading from the inside looking out. This direction is also hopefully one of your good ones. The bedroom door is very important because this is a room where you spend a lot of your time. Now you have two or three readings for the important doors where you live. In apartments, if two out of three doors face good directions then on balance your luck will probably be okay, but avoid any of them facing a Total Loss direction.

BED DIRECTION

Lastly, you need to check the bed direction. This is crucially important. You must always sleep with your head toward a good direction—not feet toward; head toward—so that the good luck hits the top of your head. This sometimes results in some rather peculiar bed orientations within the bedroom. In my mind I sometimes see a husband coming home to find the bed sticking out strangely from a corner, and saying in a despairing voice, "Oh no. She's been reading feng shui books again." We will look in more detail at the correct positioning of the bed within the bedroom in the chapters on interior geomancy.

Note that children should always sleep with their heads toward their Development direction until they are fully grown and have finished their education. This direction is definitely the best for them during this time. Incidentally, you should also make sure that wherever they sit to eat or do their homework faces their Development direction.

Now, if all those door and bed directions are auspicious for you, you are extremely lucky. It is actually quite rare for them all to be good. The easiest to change is the bed direction, although sometimes it seems impossible to find a really good orientation. You may need to change to another bedroom. You can change the orientation of a door with metal, as previously mentioned, and this does seem to work. You may be able to use an alternative entrance if confronted by one that is in your Total Loss direction. There are usually many entrances to an apartment building, and houses usually have back or side doors that may be better. Your mental attitude is surprisingly important here. You may be entering your house through the back door, but if you mentally think that this is your front door it makes a big difference. This is because you are aligning your own personal internal energy with the environmental energy of the house or apartment. It is the only situation I have come across in geomancy where you have to consciously think about it for it to work.

The biggest problem with Compass School directions arises when you discover that you and your partner are from different groups. If this is the case it does not mean that you are incompatible. Fifty percent of all couples have different groups and that does not mean that fifty percent of all couples have relationship problems. It does mean that generally one partner has trouble sleeping properly while the other is perfectly contented, one enjoys good health while the other is not so healthy, one has a successful career while the other is struggling, and so on.

If you are in the west group and your partner is in the east group, how should you orient the bed? In Chinese culture it is not unusual for partners to have different beds and even different bedrooms. One pair of extremely successful feng shui practitioners that I know have separate bedroom suites and even separate front doors to their house. In the West this is rarely an acceptable solution. People often despairingly ask me if it means that they have to sleep nose to toe, and some have even tried it. But not for long! I usually suggest that you orient the bed in one partner's "unlucky" direction. In this way, it is just a little bit unlucky for one and will be lucky for the other. It is probably better if the main breadwinner does not end up with the unlucky direction, but that is up to you.

One other tip about the bed direction—if you move your bed and you do not think there has been any change in your fortune, move it just another degree or two to the right or left. You may find that the blockage is removed.

Getting Maximum Benefit from Your Good Directions

There are many other ways in which you can use your best directions.

Always Face Your Best Directions

You should sit facing one of your good directions whenever possible. It is useful to have a small compass for a quick check when you are out and about. Always sit facing a good direction at work. This is very important as you spend a large part of your life there. Your desk should be oriented toward your wealth direction or your growth direction. If your job involves customer relationships you can try the relationships direction, although you should beware of unwanted romantic advances! You can also try this direction if you are experiencing a lot of bickering and backbiting. When you go to important meetings or negotiations, try to get there a little early to choose a seat that faces your wealth direction. You can angle your seat a little if the direction is not quite right. Try to face your health direction when you are eating. This may all sound a bit obsessive but you will be surprised how quickly it becomes a good habit.

Power from Your Best Directions

It is helpful to have the power sources for appliances such as toasters, electric kettles, microwave ovens, and rice cookers coming from the wealth or health direction. The plug or cable going into the appliance should be coming from a good direction. The direction and placement of the plug on the wall does not matter; it is the direction of the power entering the appliance that is important. So you can usually change the orientation quite easily by moving the appliance around.

Similarly, you should have the telephone cables entering the phone, fax, and computer from the wealth direction. That way you will receive good news mostly. Do this at home and at the office. Good luck comes from your good directions. People are often confused by this, so I will rephrase: the socket on the appliance should *face* the good direction and the cable should come *from* the good direction.

Travel from Your Best Directions

Another important application of the good directions is for travel. When you travel, you bring the luck of the direction that you travel *from*. So you should make that one of your best directions. It has nothing to do with the direction that you are traveling to. You bring your luck with you wherever you go. For instance, if your gua number is one and you travel from the southeast to the northwest, you bring wealth luck with you. So if are gua one and you live in Italy, business trips to the U.K. are likely to be profitable. If you are gua three, travel from the southeast to the northwest brings relationship luck, so you may have a romantic encounter!

It is not always possible to travel directly from a good direction. In this case you should stop off en route so that you end up coming from a good direction. This seems a bit extreme, but when you travel a lot you do notice the difference in your luck. The longer the journey, the bigger the difference. When I travel to Singapore from India, I try to stop off in Kuala Lumpur en route. That way, I end up coming from the north, which is my Development direction, rather than the northwest, which is the Six Killings direction.

Even traveling to work from a good direction makes a difference. It may only be a short distance, but you travel it almost every day. So it is better to live in a location that corresponds to your best direction. For example, if you are gua eight, then being located in the southwest of the city would be best. Then you would travel from the southwest to work and return home from the northeast every day.

Relocate from a Good Direction

If you are moving house, it is important to consider the implications of the travel direction. You do not want to bring bad luck with you. So if your old house is located in a bad direction relative to your new house, it is better to move to a halfway house for a few months. It is especially important not to move from a Total Loss direction. If you do not believe me, look back at all the times you have moved and check whether the move was beneficial for you or not. I don't believe the bad luck lasts for the whole of your time at the new place; it will be exhausted eventually, but by then it may be too late.

LOCATION VERSUS DIRECTION

So far I have been talking about *directions*, not *locations*, and it is sometimes easy to get them confused. I mentioned that it might be better to live in a location that corresponds to one of your good directions relative to your place of work. There are also good and bad locations within the house itself. This can become very confusing when you try to balance the advice of the three schools of geomancy. I will mention more about this later, but according to the Compass School you should have a bedroom that is in a location that corresponds to one of your good directions. For instance, if you are gua six then a bedroom located in the west, northeast, southwest, or northwest corners of the house is good. Similarly, you should locate the office or study in these places.

One last, sobering story of the power of the Total Loss direction. I visited an apartment where I had been told that the owner had had a lot of bad luck and was asked to see what I could do. As usual I checked the gua numbers of the husband, wife, and daughter. I didn't ask any sensitive questions but I gathered that the husband and wife were no longer living together. I checked the doors and the master bedroom and sure enough the bed was in the husband's Total Loss direction and the front door was in his wife's Total Loss direction. I discovered that soon after moving into the apartment the husband had lost his job and was finding it very difficult to make any progress in his career subsequently. What shocked me was that his wife had died. I felt very sad. If only he had known about the danger sooner. In my experience, the only people who can get away with always using the Total Loss direction for their bed, doors, or the direction they face while working are very strong-willed and dominant. Even then there is a serious danger of illness.

On the other hand, if you can always use your good directions as I advised, you have a much better chance of success. Please do not worry about the directions excessively—just check them for yourself and your loved ones, make any changes that are needed and forget about it.

The reason why I have explained the Compass School directions first is that I think they are by far the easiest to put into practice. All you need is your gua number and a working compass, so it is very inexpensive. You can use this information anywhere in the world to transform the whole of your life. I guarantee that you will see a difference. Whenever you decide to move house you can do so with more confidence if you know your good and bad directions. Please note however that you will find it very difficult to find a house or apartment that fulfills *all* the requirements of *all* the family members, even if you try to design one from scratch. Just do your best and don't worry about the rest. I jokingly tell my clients that after learning your ABC, next you must learn your CDE. "CDE" stands for "Can't Do Everything." Sometimes that is a very difficult lesson to learn indeed.

3

Exterior Form School Geomancy

AS I MENTIONED in the previous chapter, the front door is the mouth of the building. It is the place where the environmental energy enters. Before it enters, the energy has to be collected and encouraged to settle. If it comes slowly and meanders, it becomes heaven's breath —positive, beneficial energy. If it comes too quickly and too straight it becomes killing breath—negative, damaging energy. How can we know what type of energy is coming to our building? Firstly, you have to look at the lie of the land around the building.

In Form School geomancy there are many terms for the topographical features that are observed in the landscape, such as "falling leaves den," "reclining tiger ridge," "collapsed plum blossom," and "land of seven falling stars." This is a lifetime's study in itself and was the type of geomancy practiced by Reverend Hong Choon in Singapore. It requires a detailed knowledge of the locality and can be very effective. He said, "Topography is like psychology; when human nature is pure, so will be the fortune of the land. The human mind can shape topography; topography can influence the human mind. A good heart ensures the land will change for the better. Beneficent topography changes the human heart for the better."

This insight shows us that some land does indeed have a beneficial effect on the people that live there. This is why there are "desirable" locations in all parts of the city and the country. But it also shows us that there is always the possibility to improve the influence of the area by good land management and by always acting with good motivation.

I perform consultations in many different countries and it is not possible for me to become familiar with detailed topography. In any case most people already know where the good and bad localities are. The topography of localities changes over time. There are always up-and-coming areas, while others seem to go into decline. This is a natural, slow process that depends on the people who decide to move to the locality as much as the lie of the land itself. Usually people are aware of this process and try to invest in cheaper property in an improving area. A good Form School geomancer will be able to tell you more detail about the prospective fortunes of a particular location. However, there are some general guidelines that you can use in selecting a good area and a good location within that area.

THE ARMCHAIR CONFIGURATION

Many of the world's greatest cities are located in large basins. Think of London, Paris, Florence, Kuala Lumpur—all are surrounded by hills creating a bowl in which the positive energy can settle. Most are based on rivers that pass through the area. They are generally not exposed to strong winds. There are obvious practical reasons why a city would develop in this sort of location, but there also seems to be something more; this kind of place appears to attract positive energy.

This, of course, is looking at the lie of the land on a very large scale, but the same principles apply to smaller areas. For instance, gently undulating land contains a lot of beneficial energy; there are many small pockets in which the energy can settle, just like it settles into the large basins. The Chinese say that undulating land contains many dragons, which bring good fortune. They say this because the hills are curved like the shape of the traditional Chinese dragon; thus, the rolling countryside is full of "dragons." There are many regions that we can think of that have this topography, for example, Tuscany, southeast England, and eastern Australia. In this type of landscape it is relatively easy to find the perfect "armchair" configuration of land that is the most beneficial for the location of a house or business enterprise.

This type of land, the "armchair," has what is called a "turtle" hill behind. A turtle hill is a higher hill at the back that gives support to the house. On the left-hand side, if you were standing with your back to the turtle hill, should be a high undulating ridge called the "dragon" hill. On the right-hand side should be another ridge, one that is lower than the dragon hill. This is called the "tiger" hill. In front there should be a small hillock that acts to trap the beneficial energy in front of the front door. This is called the "phoenix" hill. In front of that there should be water—a lake or a river. The water should be flowing, not too slowly or stagnant. Even if you don't have the dragon or tiger hills, it is still very good to have a hill behind the building and water in front.

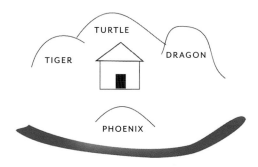

A couple of years ago I was talking to a Hollywood movie actor about geomancy and I mentioned this land configuration to him. He said, "That describes my place in New York exactly!" He has had one of the longest and most successful careers of any actor in the world. Indeed, this configuration is not difficult to spot in many of the more wealthy residences.

The Form School and Flying Star School say that ideally the house should face the south. So this places the dragon hill in the east, the tiger hill in the west, the turtle hill in the north and the phoenix hill in front in the south. The imperial palaces of China were built on this orientation. As I mentioned before, the authorities in Japan went so far as to ban the building of any other houses in that direction, thereby giving the rulers an advantage over all the subjects.

However, this southern orientation is hard to find. You may be able to find the right configuration of hills, but they will not be facing the correct direction. Don't worry too much about this; the Compass School says that if you are in the west group, then the southwest or northeast orientation is better for you, and if you are in the east group, the north orientation is also very good. The important thing is to try to find a location that has this general layout.

"But I live in a city and it is pretty flat around here," I hear you saying. That's actually fine; you can achieve this orientation with other buildings, trees, and roads, not just with hills and rivers. Your house or workplace could have a higher building behind; this becomes the turtle hill. The building on the left side as you look forward should be higher than the building on the right side, and you should have a road in front. When doing geomancy in an urban environment, we treat rivers and roads in the same way. And trees and buildings can have the same effect as hills.

This landform is like a comfortable armchair. You have a good, supportive headrest and backrest behind. There is a higher armrest on the left and a slightly lower one on the right. Then there is a footstool in front. The point of this configuration is to attract and gather the positive energy directly in front of your front door so that it is ready to enter.

What can you do if your land does not have any of these features?

Turtle Hill

As previously mentioned, there should be a supporting turtle hill behind, ideally located in a northerly direction. If you do not have such a hill, large building, or big tree behind your building, then put a wooden, metal, or ceramic turtle there, or some kind of representation of a turtle on the back wall of your building, such as a painting or bas-relief. The element and color you choose for your turtle should depend on the element that is recommended for that compass direction. You can use the cycles of elements shown in the table on the opposite page to help you.

You can also keep a live tortoise or terrapin in the north sector of the property. This is a very good geomancy tip because it gives support to the whole house or business. You only need one because that is the number associated with the north.

Location	Element
South	Red wood
Southwest	Yellow ceramic
West	White- or silver-colored metal or ceramic
Northwest	White- or silver-colored metal or ceramic
North	Blue- or black-colored metal
Northeast	Yellow ceramic
East	Green wood
Southeast	Green wood

Dragon Hill

If there is no dragon hill on the left side of the land then you can put a representation of a dragon on the eastern wall in the same way as you did for the turtle hill. It is best if your dragon is made with wood and painted green; a good option would be to paint a green dragon on the eastern wall.

Tiger Hill

The tiger hill should be on the right-hand side of the land and should be lower than the dragon hill, which is on the left side. It should ideally be located in the west. If the hill to the right of the land is higher than the hill on the left, then the tiger is said to be stronger than the dragon, and this is inauspicious. You can put a bright light on the left side of the land as long as this is in the southwest, south, or northeast. It is not advisable to have too much light in the other directions. If the tiger hill is absent or there is no corresponding building or tree, you can put a white metal tiger on the west side, or paint a white tiger on the western wall.

Phoenix Hill

The phoenix hill should be in front of the land and hopefully in the southern direction. It is just a small hillock, not a large hill, which would tend to block the energy from entering the land. If it is absent you can create a small elevation in the front of your land or place a large boulder there. The point is to create a space where the positive energy will be encouraged to settle. You can also put a red wooden bird in the south of the land.

The reasons for all the different animals, colors, and elements will be very clear to you once you understand the characteristics of the trigrams and the cycles of the elements well. I cannot emphasize enough how important it is to memorize these if you want to practice geomancy successfully.

SURROUNDING STRUCTURES AND ORIENTATION

Certain structures and buildings that are in close proximity to your land will have an effect. The magnitude of the effect depends on how big and how close they are. If other buildings or trees hide them, then you need not be concerned. Some structures are too yang and tend to give out too much energy. Some are too yin and have a negative kind of energy. Some tend to exhaust the energy of the location. Some large structures may even have a beneficial effect on your building; an experienced geomancer can determine whether this is the case or not.

You should avoid land that has the following in close proximity. They are too yang:

- ▸ Electrical transmitters and pylons
- ▸ Bridges
- ▸ Crosses and spires
- ▸ Police stations

If you live near these places you will find that there is too much energy; it is hard to find peace, quiet, and good rest.

On the other hand, the following are too yin:

- ▸ Cemeteries
- ▸ Hospitals
- ▸ Rubbish dumps
- ▸ Abandoned houses
- ▸ Prisons
- ▸ Slaughterhouses
- ▸ Polluted rivers, canals, and drains

Quite often, land that used to be used for a cemetery is used for building. The Chinese communities around the world have always taken great care in the location of their cemeteries and such land is usually very auspicious once it has been deconsecrated, but otherwise former cemeteries are to be avoided. If your building faces one of these yin influences, use a yang color such as red for the front door.

The following buildings tend to exhaust the energy of an area:

- ▸ Banks
- ▸ Schools
- ▸ Churches and temples

Apparently, banks draw in more than just your money when your house is nearby. Maybe that is why central city locations have become unpopular for homes. Schools absorb a lot of energy from the surroundings. I lived opposite one for fifteen years and can vouch for that. Temples and churches are said to exhaust the energy of the area but I think this depends on the person. I live surrounded by temples and can hardly say that it is negative; indeed it is a very positive experience.

Neighboring Rooflines and Corners

Arrow shapes are usually considered negative in geomancy; unfortunately, this is a common profile for homes. These shapes are called "poison arrows" if they face your building. It is most important that the building directly opposite your front door does not have an arrow shape. If it is at the side it is not so bad, but it's best to hide it with bushes or trees. Likewise the corner of an adjacent building should not point at your front door, as is common in apartments. If the corner is directed to the side it is not so bad. Hiding the corner with plants or bushes on a balcony would help.

This business in South Africa is giving off killing breath to the building opposite from the large arrow-shaped doorway and the cross-shaped lamppost. The lamppost is also giving negative energy to the doorway.

FENG SHUI: SEEING IS BELIEVING

Aspect

The Form School recommends that, in addition to having a southern orientation, the house should not be at the top of a hill, where it would come under the influence of strong winds. Nor should it be at the very bottom of a hill, where the energy will be stale. The land should not slope too steeply or there will be difficulty in getting the positive energy to settle. The house should not face the hillside and it should not be below the road. The site should hug the hillside and not have an exposed aspect.

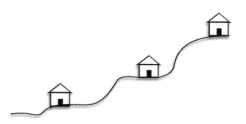

In the diagram above, the top house is too exposed. The middle house is well located but the lower house, which is at the bottom of the slope, may be too dark. It is always important to have a good balance of light and shade.

The building should not be built on exposed pillars but have a firm and closed foundation. You often find apartment buildings that have parking lots at ground level under the building that are not enclosed. In geomancy this does not give enough support.

Rivers and Roads

As I mentioned before, in general it is good to have water in front of the property and a hill behind. A river in front can be very good if it has the right shape and flow. In older times in China a lot of effort was put into finding these ideal rivers. We find these days that roads have the same effect as rivers; both have a shape, flow, and relationship to the land. All the information I will give you here applies equally to roads and rivers.

Rivers should not flow too fast past the front gate—and roads should not have rushing traffic—otherwise it is difficult to get the beneficial energy to enter and settle. Likewise, the energy tends to stagnate and become negative in front of motionless water or in a dead-end road. It is especially bad if the land is at the very end of the cul-de-sac.

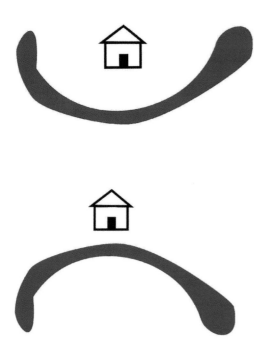

Ideally the river or road should embrace the land; the building should be on the inside of a river bend rather than the outside. The river should flow past the front of the land from left to right if it faces one of the cardinal directions (north, south, east, or west). If the land faces one of the secondary directions (northeast, southeast, southwest, or northwest) then the flow should be from right to left. A road often slopes from one end to the other past the land so this can be taken as the direction of flow.

The building should not face the outside of the bend of the road or river, which becomes like a bow being aimed at your property.

A river or road behind the land is also not good because water (or traffic) does not give the support that is required there.

FENG SHUI: SEEING IS BELIEVING

A "T" junction facing the land is not good. If the environmental energy travels in straight lines, it comes to the land too fast and becomes a negative poison arrow. So a road or river that faces the front of the land directly in this way brings negative energy—the longer and straighter the river or road, the worse the effect. This is especially bad if it is opposite the front door. If this is the case, you can put the front gate to one side so that it does not directly face the road or river and hide the road or river from the front door with trees and shrubs.

A "Y" junction is also not good. Again, try to have the front gate located away from the junction and hide it from the front door with foliage.

It is better not to have a plot of land on the corner of two rivers or roads. You can build a fence or plant tall bushes and trees to hide the road on one side so that the facing direction is more clear.

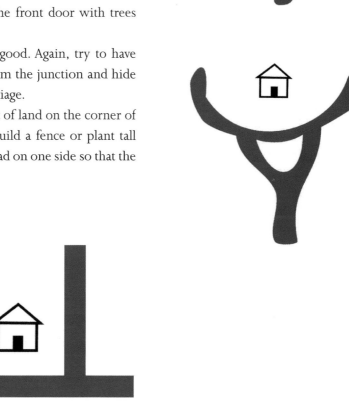

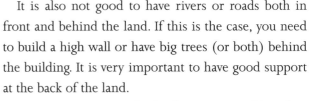

It is also not good to have rivers or roads both in front and behind the land. If this is the case, you need to build a high wall or have big trees (or both) behind the building. It is very important to have good support at the back of the land.

An overpass next to the land is negative, although it is better if it embraces the building rather than faces it. You often see this in cities, which have many raised roadways and railways. You can observe how quickly adjacent properties deteriorate after they are built. In Singapore they are making a concerted effort to cover all these structures with foliage, thereby softening their effect on the surroundings.

Dragon Path

It is also good to have what is called a "dragon path" in your garden. This is a winding pathway that is located on the "dragon" side of your garden: the left side if you are facing the front of the land, or the eastern side. The path can be constructed from flat stones bounded on each side by low flowering plants. You can also use lights on each side to guide the positive energy. The path should lead along the side of the house to the front door. You only need a space about ten feet wide to do this.

Gates

Gates can be quite high, five feet or more. It does not seem to matter if they are solid or made of a grille. If the gate is a grille, then try not to have cross shapes in the design. A curved design is better. If you have arrow shapes on the gate, make sure they point upward, not downward, and they must not be in a direct line with your front door. Be careful that they do not fire poison arrows at your neighbor; make sure that the gate does not face the opposite neighbor's gate directly.

It is good if the gateposts have lamps on top to attract good environmental energy. It is also effective to have animal statues on each post in the form of lions, eagles, and so on. This offers protection to the land. In Chinese communities, you often see fierce-looking ceramic dogs on the gateposts. They often look a bit battered and broken. This is said to be because they have absorbed what would otherwise have been bad luck.

Driveways

In the same way that it is not good to have a straight road pointing toward your land, you should not have a straight driveway leading to the front door; when the environmental energy travels in straight lines it becomes a poison arrow, negative killing breath. So it is better if the driveway curves or meanders. That way the energy is slowed down and becomes beneficial heaven's breath.

At Windsor Castle, the home of the royal family of England, there is a three-mile-long, dead-straight ceremonial driveway that leads directly to the castle through Windsor Great Park. You can imagine how much killing breath is generated. It is curious that we use the expression "dead-straight" in English, with its rather negative connotation.

The geomancy cure for straight driveways is to put a round feature in front of the house. The Windsors have constructed a large sculpture on a roundabout in front of Buckingham Palace in London, which is situated at the end of another long driveway called the Mall. This slows down the energy so it is no longer negative.

It is good if the driveway or path broadens out as it reaches the front gate. This creates a funnel effect to guide the beneficial energy. It is also okay to have a driveway with a separate entrance and exit.

The best driveways meander and are lined with shrubs or hedges. Trees are good as long as they are not overwhelming. It seems that heaven's breath is attracted to archways, so an archway of shrubs over the gate is very good. A line of low small lights on each side of the driveway is very good for guiding the energy at night.

Boundary Walls and Fences

The wall in the picture below is one of the most extraordinary I have ever seen. I asked a lady in the house next-door who lived there. "That is the doctor's house," she replied, "but he died two months ago." Frankly, I was not surprised to hear of the poor man's fate. A house should not be like a prison. The point of having walls and fences is to demarcate the boundary of the land, to give

privacy, and to offer some protection from intruders, but this should not be at the expense of keeping out the beneficial environmental energy. There was no way any good energy could get into this land, past the huge spikes and the despairing men.

A solid, fairly high wall is a good feature to have at the back of the land. It gives support behind the building and can represent the turtle hill if it is missing. You can also use walls to block out and hide the negative environmental features that I explained before, such as electrical transformers and transmitters, cemeteries, and polluted rivers and drains. But it is not so good to have high walls at the side and at the front of the building, because they can prevent heaven's breath from entering. It is better if the walls, fences, or hedges are lower and porous rather than solid, especially if the land is quite small.

You often see barbed wire and broken glass on walls. These give off a lot of killing breath from all the little spikes and sharp edges. I really cannot see the point of having them. They will not deter people who are absolutely intent on getting in. Either remove them completely or cover them with foliage from climbing plants or bushes inside the wall. Thorny plants such as bougainvillea, climbing roses, and blackthorn are okay as long as they have foliage that covers the thorns.

BUILDING PROFILE

Many office and apartment blocks have a rectangular profile and in general this is considered an auspicious shape. This is because in the table of the trigrams the rectangle shape is associated with wood, and wood is associated with growth. So it is good for both businesses and homes. If the building tapers toward the top this is also auspicious. An example of this is the Empire State Building in New York.

It has always been well known in Chinese feng shui that two identical towers are not auspicious—indeed I have warned students about the dangers of twin towers since my very first courses. Nowadays of course twin towers have taken a whole new negative meaning and this is a traumatic subject for many. However, it is important to analyse this phenomenon in some detail.

The Chinese are superstitious about twin towers because they look like the two joss sticks that they offer to ancestors, but there are more subtle reasons to avoid building them. If you look at the table of the trigrams and their characteristics, you can see that the number two is associated with Kun, which is the most yin of the trigrams. The number two has a negative connotation in Flying Star geomancy, usually foreboding sickness, and is also associated with the element "big earth."

In the case of the towers of the World Trade Center, the situation was made worse because they had square-shaped bases, which is also associated with the earth element. Earth is generally considered to be yin in nature. Also, the corners of the towers were pointing directly at each other, creating very powerful poison arrows. Additionally, the attacks took place in September—"between" summer and autumn, which is also associated with Kun. It seems that this extremely heavy combination of very yin influences was too much for the buildings to sustain. The negative energy of the site, now known as "ground zero," was palpable for years after the terrible event. The building of the Freedom Tower at the site will go a long way to restoring good energy. This new tower has a modified octagonal shape, which is well known to have protective properties, as I will explain later.

I am sometimes asked if a similar fate awaits the famous twin towers of Kuala Lumpur—until recently, the world's tallest buildings. The prognosis is a bit more optimistic in this case. Indeed there are two towers, but they are joined by a bridge at about one-third of the height, which may help. The footprint shape of the towers is based on the eight-sided Ba Gua. In addition, the towers are mostly clad in metal; in the cycle of elements metal exhausts earth, so the heavy earth influence is somewhat reduced. "Big metal" is associated with Qian, which is the most yang trigram, and in this way the yin and yang influences of the towers are balanced. On the negative side, the towers have a lot of corners that are firing poison arrows in all directions and also at each other. So from this analysis there seems to be less danger to the Kuala Lumpur towers than there was to the New York ones. Would I live anywhere near them? No way!

In general, the conventional, triangular style of roofline is considered auspicious. The upward-pointing arrow shapes symbolize growth and upward movement, although, as I mentioned earlier, sometimes they can be poison arrows for neighboring buildings. You should also beware of having downward-pointing arrow designs above the front door.

These triangular roofs attract yang energy; the triangle shape is associated with the fire element and is thus considered very yang. An example of a very yang-shaped roofline is the Sydney Opera House. One may think that a building with a roof that represents the fire element and juts out into a large expanse of water such as Sydney Harbour would suffer from an imbalance of the fire and water elements. However, this is clearly not the case. An opera star I asked about the building praised its energy compared to other opera houses. She said that it has a wonderful energy for performers and they enjoy singing there very much, even though the theater itself leaves a lot to be desired in terms of acoustic and backstage conditions. The Opera House brings the fire element into the water in a supportive or "friend" relationship in the cycles of elements. The fire energizes the water, symbolically producing steam. This must be why the artists feel energized when they perform there. I always find it a

great place to go to when I am feeling a bit down. If there was less water then the fire element would be too strong and the balance would not be so good.

An example of a building with a very negative profile in Australia is the Newcastle City Council administration office block. Locally it is known as the "mushroom" because of its top-heavy shape with the belly cut out. It does not have proper support, and as this is a community building, support for the community seems to have been undermined. It may be just a coincidence, but not long after the building was constructed there was a terrible earthquake in the city. Large earthquakes are very rare in Australia and this was one of the worst ever in Australian history, in which many people lost their lives.

Pyramid shapes are said to be very yin, mainly due to their funeral connotation—their association with the pyramid tombs of Egypt. So you would not want to build a house with this shape; nor would you want to have a square-

FENG SHUI: SEEING IS BELIEVING

based pyramid shape on the roof. However, this shape is okay for buildings with more yin purposes—such as museums. A good example of a place where this has been very successful is the Louvre in Paris.

When it was first proposed, putting a glass pyramid in the heart of such an old building seemed a very radical design indeed, but from a geomancy point of view it was an inspired move and contributed greatly to the success of the museum. The pyramid is a yin shape but it has been constructed from glass, which gives balancing yang light energy. It also brought a square-shaped footprint into the extremely large U-shaped empty space between the wings of the museum. The square shape is associated with the earth element, and hence provides the overall supporting energy that was missing at the center of the original design. The glass used in the construction is also associated with the earth element. The triangular shapes of each side of the pyramid represent the fire element, which produces earth in the productive cycle of the elements. So the energy of the whole building became much better balanced.

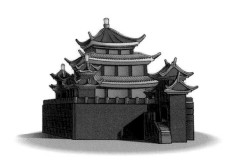

Chinese temple roofs have a curve at each corner, pointing to the heavens. In this way, neighboring buildings are not hit by poison arrows from the roofline. This style of roof is also common in a lot of other countries, so this seems to be common wisdom.

A dome-shaped roof, such as that of the Taj Mahal in India, is rather yin in character and is good for places of worship. The famous Millenium Dome in London, on the other hand, is not popular at all and nobody seems to know quite what to do with it; the dome shape does not provide enough yang energy for the shows and exhibitions it was meant to house and so it is unlikely to be successful for these purposes. Additionally, the building is almost completely surrounded by a sweeping curve of the River Thames—this is like a hangman's noose, symbolically strangling the site.

4

Exterior Compass School Geomancy

I**N THE PREVIOUS CHAPTER** I explained the recommendations of the Form School with regard to the larger local environment. In this chapter we will look more closely at the plot of land itself and the recommendations of the Compass School, including the crucial role that the Lo Shu square and the Ba Gua play in successful exterior geomancy.

LAND SHAPE

It is generally agreed in geomancy that the best shape for a plot of land is a regular rectangle or square. The best placement of the house is in the back half of the land. This is so that the front part can be used to allow the heaven's breath energy to settle. In many European countries it is common to see the front of the house close to the road at the front of the land; it seems that people value their back garden more than having a front garden. But it is important to have a reasonably sized front garden because otherwise there is nowhere for

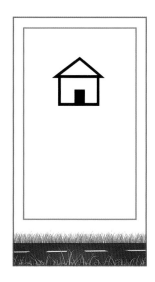

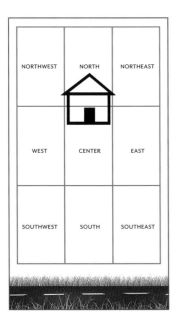

the good energy to collect and settle; it will just continue down the road past your door and pass you by.

Applying the Lo Shu Square to the Land

In chapter 1, I mentioned that the combination of the Later Heaven Ba Gua arrangement of the trigrams and the sequence of numbers in the Lo Shu square is very important in determining what elements should be placed in what sector of the land and of the house. The first step in this process is applying the Lo Shu square to the layout of the land as shown to the left.

The land must be divided into nine equal sectors. To do this you divide each side into thirds and join up the lines. In first example on the left, the land faces the auspicious southern direction.

If your land faces a different direction then you simply put that one at the front of your diagram and allocate the other directions to their respective places. In the second example the land faces southwest. It is not always as easy to apply the Lo Shu square as it sounds because many plots of land are an irregular shape.

In chapter 2, I explained how to determine which Compass School group you belong to: east or west. The Form School recommends the south direction as best, but if you belong to the west group then this is one of your bad directions. In this case, the Compass School overrides the Form School recommendation and if you belong to the west group then it is better to have land that faces southwest or northeast.

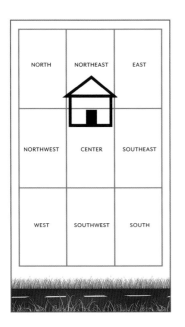

Alternative Layout of the Sectors

Another way to determine the location of the sectors is to apply the compass rose directly to the layout of the property. This gives more or less the same result as applying the Lo Shu square; the main difference is that there is no central sector. This method can be useful for strangely shaped land or buildings, though in general I prefer using the Lo Shu square.

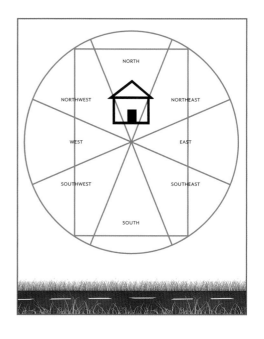

Missing Corners

In chapter 1, I discussed the trigrams and their corresponding locations. The table below will show you what type of luck is influenced in each area. This is especially important if the land is irregular and there is a missing sector. I will explain each type of luck and how to enhance it a little later.

SE Wealth	S Reputation	SW Relationships
E Health	Center Support	W Children
NE Knowledge	N Career	NW Mentors

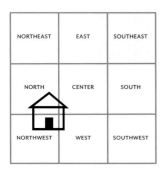

Missing corner

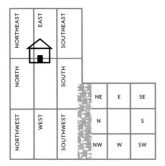

Missing corner with fence

T-shape

If the plot of land is L-shaped then when you apply the Lo Shu square grid there may be one or more missing corners. In the example to the left, the southeast corner is missing so wealth luck would be adversely affected. Also, the corner of the land is pointing directly at the house, which is negative. The house must be positioned toward the back of the land.

If the land is big enough, you can fix this problem by squaring it off with a fence, wall, hedge, or line of trees and shrubs no less than five feet high, as demonstrated by the second example. Then you can treat the two areas as if they were separate for geomancy purposes and neither area has missing corners.

If the land is T-shaped then there may be more than one missing corner. In the third example to the left, the southeast is mostly missing and the southwest corner is completely missing; both wealth and relationships would be adversely affected. Again, you could fix this problem by putting a fence or hedge across the base of the T to create two separate regular rectangles.

Protruding Corners

If part of the land is extended a little in one sector, if one of the corners protrudes, this is said to enhance the luck of that sector. In the example on the opposite page, the northwest sector is protruding, so mentor luck would be enhanced. However, if the corner protrudes more than one third of the total length or width of the land, a missing corner is created.

Irregularly Shaped Land

In general it is always better to locate the building in the rear half of the land, regardless of the shape. This is in order to have space before the front door where the beneficial energy can accumulate. However, there are a few exceptions for some irregularly shaped land.

If the land is an extremely irregular shape, try to create a regular rectangle by using fences, hedges, or shrubs, and position the building toward the back of the new rectangle.

Triangular-shaped land is really no good. It is difficult to create a rectangular space within it unless it is very large. The building should be located facing the longest side of the triangle.

If the land is parallelogram shaped, then the house should be located at the front or the middle rather than at the back.

The Five Elements

Each sector of the Lo Shu square is enhanced by the presence of one of the five elements: water, wood, fire, earth and metal. The absence of the enhancing element or the presence of negative elements causes problems with the luck of each sector, as I will explain shortly.

Water

Water can be represented on your land by a pond, swimming pool, fountain, or water tank. You can also represent water with wavy shapes or the colors black and blue, which are associated with water. You must be careful wherever you put water features; they should not be so large that they overwhelm the house, so a swimming pool should be in proportion. Water should always be kept moving. You can recycle the water, but make sure it is kept clean.

Water is often associated with wealth in geomancy and it is important that the overall flow is toward the house, especially if the water is in front of the front door. This represents wealth coming in. A fountain that sprays water in all directions is no good; wealth

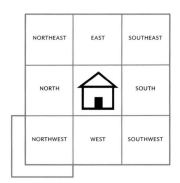

Protruding corner

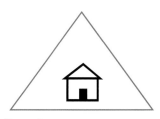

Irregular

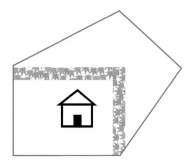

Triangular

Parallelogram

Infinity pool

would come in and go out just as quickly. It is better to have a small waterfall with the direction of flow toward the house. For example, the "infinity"-style swimming pool, where the water appears to drop away from the land into the horizon, looks very nice—but unfortunately all that water flowing away from the house is a problem.

Water should be situated to the left of the front door as you look out, where it brings prosperity. It should not be on the right as this is said to cause the man of the house to have a wandering eye. Water should only be in front of the house, not behind because this goes against the armchair configuration of land recommended in the Form School; water does not give the support needed behind the house. If there is water both behind and in front it is said to be negative for young children. It should also not be on a higher level of land than the house.

Some masters consider it very negative to have water above you, such as a rooftop swimming pool or a water tank above your bedroom. Even a blue or black-colored roof is inauspicious. It symbolizes "water on the mountain," which is the name of a very unstable configuration; when you combine the trigrams for water (Kan) and mountain (Gen) it gives the hexagram Jian, which means "hardship." There would be difficulty in making progress in your life if you live under a pool. It would be like having some kind of disability.

Wood

Wood is usually well represented on the land by trees, plants, hedges and fences, garden furniture, and wooden sheds. There are two types of wood in the table of the trigrams: big and small. Small wood refers to flowers, small plants, and small wooden objects, and is associated with the color light green. Big wood refers to trees and larger wooden garden structures such as pergolas and gazebos, and is associated with darker green. Wood is also represented by rectangular shapes.

Trees such as pines and cypress, which are arrow shaped, are okay if they are not in front of the house where they may send poison arrows to the front door. Wood represents growth so it is important to regularly clear out all dead wood and plants, so that they don't attract yin energy. Succulent plants are very good because they contain a lot of water, which is productive for wood. Cacti are very prickly and all those little spines give off negative energy. They are okay outside, where they give protection, but never keep them inside.

As I mentioned before, trees can represent your dragon, tiger, and turtle hills if they are missing. However, try not to have the trees overhang and overwhelm the house. They should always be kept in good proportion to the land and the house.

Fire

Fire can be represented by a number of things on your land; it could be a bright lamp, garden incinerator, or barbeque. The shape associated with the fire element is the triangle and the color is red. It would be good to have red flowers. Triangular-shaped objects are good, as long as they are not poison arrows pointing at the front door.

Earth

There are two types of earth element, big earth and small earth. Big earth is represented by rocks and boulders, large pieces of marble such as statues, large earthenware pots or urns, paving stones, patios, and concrete areas. Small earth is represented by smaller pots, pebbles, small ceramic figures, crystals, and small areas of gravel or sand. They are associated with the square shape and the earth colors; ocher, terracotta, brown, and so on.

Metal

There are also two types of metal—big and small. Big metal is represented by metal railings and gates, metal lampposts and garden tools; small metal by wind chimes, metal mobiles, and bells. The colors associated with metal are white and metallic. The shape associated with metal is the circle. Wind chimes are recommended in many different situations in geomancy. They are very effective in enhancing the metal sectors and in controlling negative Flying Star School influences. Wind chimes should always have five or six hollow metal tubes. Five represents the earth element, which produces metal in the productive cycle, and six represents the metal element itself. Solid rods do not work so well. It is best if they are hanging from a circular piece of metal or wood. The wind chime pictured here is a good one.

THE EFFECTS OF THE ELEMENTS ON YOUR LUCK

When you have applied the Lo Shu square to the land, you can then start to enhance each of the nine types of luck in their respective sectors by putting the right elements in the right places. Let me remind you of the four cycles of the elements:

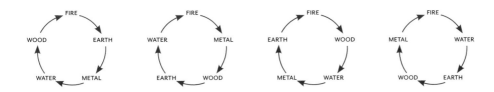

The table of the trigrams in chapter 1 shows the main element that will enhance the luck of each sector. With that information, you can use the cycles of the elements to deduce the productive and supportive elements for each sector, as shown here.

SE **Wealth**	S **Reputation**	SW **Relationships**
Enhanced by small wood *Produced by* water *Supported by* small earth	*Enhanced by* fire *Produced by* wood *Supported by* small metal	*Enhanced by* big earth *Produced by* fire *Supported by* small water
E **Health**	Center **Support**	W **Children**
Enhanced by big wood *Produced by* water *Supported by* small earth	*Enhanced by* earth *Produced by* fire *Supported by* small water	*Enhanced by* small metal *Produced by* earth *Supported by* small wood
NE **Knowledge**	N **Career**	NW **Mentors**
Enhanced by small earth *Produced by* fire *Supported by* small water	*Enhanced by* water *Produced by* metal *Supported by* small fire	*Enhanced by* big metal *Produced by* earth *Supported by* small wood

For example, wealth luck is influenced in the southeast of the land. Its main element—the element that enhances it—is "small wood": flowers and shrubs and so on. It is also produced or helped by water, and it is supported by small amounts of earth element—ceramics, pots, crystals, and so on.

There are also two elements that must be avoided in each sector. These come from the destructive and exhaustive cycles of the elements. The elements that damage the wealth luck of the southeast sector are metal and fire; metal cuts wood in the destructive cycle, and fire uses up wood in the exhaustive cycle.

SE **Wood** *Destroyed by* metal *Exhausted by* fire	S **Reputation** *Destroyed by* water *Exhausted by* earth	SW **Relationships** *Destroyed by* wood *Exhausted by* metal
E **Health** *Destroyed by* metal *Exhausted by* fire	Center **Support** *Destroyed by* wood *Exhausted by* metal	W **Children** *Destroyed by* fire *Exhausted by* water
NE **Knowledge** *Destroyed by* wood *Exhausted by* metal	N **Career** *Destroyed by* earth *Exhausted by* wood	NW **Mentors** *Destroyed by* fire *Exhausted by* water

Now you can see why it is so important to memorize the cycles of the elements. If you do, then when you look at any object on your land or in your house, you can tell whether it is helpful or harmful.

You can use large amounts of the main element and the productive element in each sector; for instance, a bright lamp in the southwest will help relationship luck. However, you should not use large amounts of the element from the supportive cycle. A little water in the southwest can help to make the earth element fertile; too much will make relationships very muddy. You should avoid the destructive-cycle elements altogether, or at least keep them to a minimum; they are always harmful. This means that it is not good to have large plants and trees in the southwest of the land. Likewise the element from the exhaustive cycle will deplete the luck of the sector, so too much metal in the southwest will affect relationship luck adversely.

Now I will explain in detail the effect of each element on each of the nine types of luck.

Reputation

The southern sector of the land influences reputation and fame. If you are suffering from unkind gossip or feeling undervalued, or if your business is not becoming well known and respected, then you may have a problem in this sector.

The table of the trigrams in chapter 1 shows that the element associated with the south is fire. That means that the main element to enhance your reputation is fire, so first of all you should have at least one bright light here. Three or four lights would be good because those are the numbers of the wood element, which produces fire in the productive cycle. Put the light or lights on a wooden pole about five feet tall and keep it on at least eight hours a day. The lamp casing should have a triangular-shaped top because the triangle is associated with fire and represents growth and upward movement. The lamppost is better made from wood than concrete because the earth element exhausts fire energy. Metal is a friend to fire in the supportive cycle, so a metal lamppost is also okay.

You can also have a lot of wood in the southern sector, so trees are good. If the land faces south, however, remember to make sure that they are not in front of the front door and are not inhibiting heaven's breath from entering the land. You can use other objects made from wood, such as fencing, flower boxes, garden furniture, and so on. Use green and red colors in this sector; for example you could plant red flowers. Rectangular-shaped objects are good.

You must avoid having water features such as swimming pools in the south because water destroys fire in the destructive cycle of the elements. Do not have blue flowers here or any wavy-shaped objects, as these are associated with water. You should also avoid having the earth element; rocks, concrete, earth colors, square-shaped objects, and so on, because this exhausts fire energy.

Relationships

During my consultations I usually ask my clients if there are any particular problems that they would like to try to deal with using geomancy. Relationship problems are usually at the top of the list, closely followed by money worries. It seems that at this time in our world we most need to learn how to form stable relationships and maintain them; not just between man and woman but between friends, nations, ideologies, and religions. So much suffering is caused by the attitude that others are here to help us, rather than the opposite. Anyway, geomancy has much to offer in the way of improving relationship luck, and as I jokingly tell my clients, "I can guarantee interest but not necessarily quality!"

If you or your family members are having marriage problems, problems finding a partner, disharmony in the house or at work, loneliness and lack of friends, or the feeling that people seem to be against you, you must look at the southwest sector and see what elements you have there.

The main element of the southwest is big earth: large rocks and boulders, concrete, gravel or sand, large stone sculptures, and large earthenware pots. The color for this sector is ocher and other earth colors; the shape is square.

Fire is the element that is productive for earth, so you can have lights, red colors, and triangle shapes to help relationship luck. It is very effective to have a lamp, but probably better if it is not red! It should be on a post that is about five feet tall and made from concrete, stone, or plastic. The top casing can be triangle shaped, like the lamp for the southern sector. A friend of mine had a lamp like this in the southwest of her garden, which she used humorously to interfere with her daughter's love life. When her daughter had trouble finding a boyfriend, she would turn on the lamp. When a boy would come to take her daughter out, she would turn the lamp off if she didn't like him. She repeated the process until her daughter found a partner she approved of and now she is happily married.

It is okay to have a little water in the southwest sector, as it has a friend relationship with earth in the supportive cycle. But, as is the case with all the supportive cycle elements, it is better not to overdo the amount. As I mentioned before, if there is too much water in the southwest then relationships can get very muddy and complicated.

You must avoid having the wood element in the southwest. Wood destroys earth in the destructive cycle of elements. This is difficult in a garden, but you should try to keep it to a minimum. There should be no large trees, and flowers should be red or yellow. This makes the southwest the perfect place for a rock garden or a Zen-style garden made primarily of rocks, gravel, and raked sand. You must also avoid having metal here. Metal depletes earth luck in the exhaustive cycle of the elements.

Children

The sector that affects the luck of the children of the house is in the west. If your children are having difficulty with health, school, and so on, or you are experiencing difficulty in having children in the first place, you must check the elements in the west of your land.

The main element here is small metal, so you can have wind chimes and other metal mobiles, small metal sculptures, or metal bowls and bells. I have often found that placing one or more wind chimes with six hollow metal tubes is extremely effective. The best color is white or metallic colors such as gold, silver, or copper. The best shape is the circle. Metal is produced by earth in the productive cycle so you can have pots, stone statues, gravel, square shapes, earth colors, and so on. It is supported by wood so it is okay to have plants here but probably better not to have large trees. You can paint a white tiger on the wall here, but make sure you have a green dragon on the eastern wall first to provide balance.

You should avoid the fire element as this destroys metal in the destructive cycle, so no bright lights or red color. The element that exhausts metal is water so you must avoid having pools and ponds, blue or black colors, or wavy shapes in the western sector.

Mentors

The northwest sector is associated with the luck of mentors. Everyone needs help from those who are knowledgeable and skilled, but it is not easy to find people who are willing to help us to grow. A mentor could be someone who takes an interest in your career, a school or college teacher, a spiritual guide, a sports coach, or just someone willing to give good advice. If you feel you are not getting enough help and encouragement in your work or study, or feel you are not making spiritual progress, then you need to look at the elements in the northwest of the land.

The main element to enhance mentor luck is big metal; large wind chimes with five or six hollow tubes, metal sculptures, large metal decorative pots, a metal shed and garden tools, and so on. White and metallic colors, and round objects are good.

Metal is produced by earth in the productive cycle so you can have pots, stone statues, gravel, square shapes, earth colors, and so on. Again, metal is supported by wood, so white-flowered plants are okay but it is better not to have large trees.

Fire destroys metal in the destructive cycle. You must avoid having the fire element here, so no bright lights, incinerators, or barbeques. Avoid red color and triangular shapes. In the exhaustive cycle, water exhausts metal, so no pools, ponds, or other water features. Avoid having blue or black colors, or wavy shapes here.

Career

Career luck is influenced by the northern sector of the land. If you are having trouble getting the job or important promotion that you want or you just seem to be stagnating in a particular job, then you must check the elements in the north. Activating this sector should remove blockages to career progress, or may even trigger a move to a completely new career; you have to have a mind that is open to new opportunities when they come.

This is, unfortunately, a complicated sector. The main element of the northern sector is water, but the Form School recommends that the land face south and also says that you should not have water behind the house, in the north. So if your house faces south, it is best to put metal objects in the north, because metal produces water in the productive cycle of the elements. You should also keep a turtle here in a metal bowl of water. A turtle made of metal is very good in this location.

If your land faces any of the other directions you can have a water feature such as a pond or swimming pool in the northern sector, but keep it in proportion to the land; it shouldn't be too overwhelming. A swimming pool should be shaped to embrace the house, not curve out toward it. Just one water feature is enough as one is the number associated with the north. Make sure that the water is active and that the general flow is toward the house. Blue and black colors and wavy shapes are good. You can also have metal objects here, as previously mentioned. Fire is a friend to water in the supportive cycle, so small lights are okay.

You must avoid the earth element, which destroys water in the destructive cycle. Do not have large pots, areas of concrete, stone sculptures, and so on. Wood depletes water in the exhaustive cycle, so minimize the number of trees and large plants. Blue flowers are okay. Avoid square and rectangular-shaped objects, as well as green and earth colors.

Knowledge

The northeast sector affects knowledge luck. If you or your family members are having trouble with study, acquiring knowledge, passing examinations, and so on, you must check the elements in the northeast of your land.

The main element is small earth, so you should have small pots and ceramics, small decorative rocks, crystals, and small stone sculptures. Earth colors and square shapes are good. In the productive cycle, earth is produced by fire, so you can have lamps in this sector as well as red-colored and triangular-shaped objects. Earth is supported by water so you can have a small pond or birdbath here. Be very careful not to overdo the amount of water.

In the destructive cycle, earth is destroyed by wood, so it is better not to have trees. As with the southwest sector, this is a good place to have a Zen-style garden made primarily of rocks, gravel, and sand. It is better not to have any plants as even small wood can damage small earth. If you must have some plants, then make sure they are low and small, and have red, yellow, or orange flowers.

Health

It is rather curious that health concerns usually come third after wealth and relationships when I do consultations. When people think about it seriously, though, they realize that their health is really the most important. It is also one of the most difficult types of luck to activate. Bad health, once acquired, is very difficult to deal with, so it is doubly important that you protect and enhance the eastern sector of your land. According to Buddhism, the cause of health is nonviolence, particularly not killing even small animals and insects. It is particularly beneficial to save animals from harm by rescuing those that would otherwise be killed.

The main element for the eastern sector is big wood, so it very important to have large trees here. Three are enough as that is the number associated with the east. The eastern side corresponds to the dragon hill, if your house faces the recommended southern direction, so it is okay to have big trees on this side of the house. However, if the east is on the right-hand side of your land, you should place large wooden objects instead: wooden sculptures, heavy wooden garden furniture, a gazebo or pergola, wooden barrels with large plants, and so on. Remember that arrow-shaped trees such as cypress and pine are good as long as they do not face the front door. Green colors and rectangular-shaped objects are good. Wood is produced by water, so this is a good place for a large water feature such as a swimming pool or fountain. As in the previous example, make sure that the fountain flows toward the house. If you have a pond or irregular pool, ensure that it embraces the house.

It is good to have an image of a green dragon in the east of your land, where it will attract a very positive energy. You can have lots of plants in this sector, particularly ones with blue flowers. Earth is a friend to wood in the supportive cycle, so you can have the same earth-element features as I mentioned for the northeast sector. Avoid metal, which destroys wood in the destructive cycle. Also avoid the fire element, which exhausts wood; do not have lamps in this sector.

Wealth

Wealth luck is influenced by the southeastern sector of the land. It is rare for people to tell me that they have enough wealth; usually we can do with more. Please remember that wealth has a cause, which is generosity and altruism; you cannot get something for nothing.

The main element of the southeast is small wood; small plants, shrubs and flowers, wooden wind chimes with four or five tubes, and other small wooden objects. The best shape for this sector is the rectangle and the best color is light green. The plant growth in this area should be luxuriant but not overwhelming: a garden but not a jungle. Keep it free of dead leaves and plants. As with the health sector in the east, water is productive here. A small fountain, pond, or pool can be very effective here. Again, it is very good to have a lot of blue flowers in the southeast sector. Small earth-element features are also good. As with the eastern sector, avoid metal, which cuts wood energy, and fire, which exhausts it.

Support

The central sector is associated with support for the whole house, family, or business enterprise. So if you feel that your overall situation is unstable or not progressing as you would like, then you must check the elements here. The main element for the center is earth and the recommendations for the productive, supportive, destructive, and exhaustive elements are the same as for the southwest and the northeast sectors.

Do not have a large empty area in the center of the land. Make sure that the earth element is present, or at least that there are strongly defined square shapes. Five squares are good because five is the number associated with the central sector. Do not have large amounts of the wood element here or you will destroy support luck. Similarly, metal will exhaust it. Bright lamps are good in this sector because they produce earth-element energy. I do not recommend having any water here as it is a fluid, changeable element and may reduce the stability that we are trying to achieve.

That concludes our look at the external environment and the effect it may have on your fortunes. Next we will look at the importance of the front door and ways of protecting your building from negative influences.

5

The Front Door and the Floor Plan

ONCE YOU HAVE gathered the positive energy in front of the building, you must encourage it to enter. The front door is the mouth of the building through which the energy enters, so it is extremely important. Indeed, the front door is the most crucial aspect of geomancy to get right because the luck of the whole building depends on it.

It is very important that you protect your home or business premises, and in particular the front door, from poison arrows and inauspicious neighboring buildings and other structures. I described these in detail in chapter 3. As you stand inside your front door, looking outside, what can you see? You do not want to see any of the negative buildings and structures that I have mentioned: a radio transmitter, a bridge, a hospital, and so on. You do not want to see a straight pole, pillar, or tree trunk; it is surprising how many houses, apartments, and shops have pillars directly in front of the front door. You do not want to see cross shapes or corners of buildings or walls directly facing the door. You do not want to see a long, dead-straight road, driveway, or path leading to the front door. You do not want to see upward-pointing arrow shapes from rooflines, trees, or fences.

Defensive and Aggressive Protection

I have already mentioned some defensive techniques against the negative killing breath energy that inauspicious structures cause, and I will go into greater detail about them here. I shall also explain some aggressive techniques so that you are aware of others who may use them and can protect your property from them, but I do not recommend that you use them yourself.

Defensive Techniques

You can remodel poison arrows that are within your control, such as straight paths and driveways and trees that are on your property. To deal with inauspicious objects that are outside of your control, such as structures on neighboring land, you must try to disguise and hide them using trees, shrubs, walls, and

fences. If you cannot see them from the front door, they cannot harm you. Remember that killing breath travels fast and in straight lines, so what you can't see you don't have to worry about. Protect the sides and back of your building as much as you can, but the front door is the most important.

I must stress that the only structures that are cause for concern are very obvious and fairly close. If they are small and far away, you need not worry so much about obscuring them. Though if you are not sure what is too large, or small enough not to be concerned about, it is always best to err on the side of caution. If there is nothing you can do, then don't worry about it; you just have to live with it and use as many of the other geomancy techniques as you can to help overcome problems.

You can have statues of protecting animals such as lions, elephants, and eagles on each side of the front door, as well as on the gateposts. You should not have representations of fierce animals inside the building, only outside. Umbrellas represent protection, so it is good to have an umbrella stand outside and to one side of the front door. Cacti are said to offer protection, but do not have them in front of the front door. I do not recommend this kind of protection for businesses where you are trying to attract customers from the street, such as hotels, restaurants, and shops. The sight of a fierce lion may put them off!

Aggressive Techniques

The Power of the Ba Gua

An example of a very powerful protective symbol is the Ba Gua mirror. A Ba Gua mirror is an Early Heaven Ba Gua with a concave or convex mirror in the center, where the yin/yang symbol usually is. In a Ba Gua mirror, the Early Heaven arrangement of the trigrams is more powerful than the Later Heaven arrangement. This is extremely powerful but it is also very aggressive because it reflects whatever negative energy is coming to the mirror directly back where it came from. I do not recommend that you use this kind of mirror anywhere as it always causes some harm to others and in the long run this is not to your own benefit. It is much better to use defensive techniques to overcome problems.

Even without the mirror, a Ba Gua has a lot of power. Some friends of mine came across this rather extraordinary gate in Delhi. The property apparently belonged to a rather secretive sect that did not want to be disturbed. The two Ba Guas would certainly have that effect. The sad thing was that I was told the Hindu priest who lived opposite had contracted cancer.

In Sydney, another friend gave me a lift in his car and I noticed that there was a Ba Gua dangling from the rear view mirror. I asked him why he had it and he told me he had read some feng shui books and it was for protection. I asked him if he had had any problems since he started using it. He told me that he had had two small accidents that needed bodywork repairs. After the second accident the owners of the body repair shop gave him a temporary car and he took his Ba Gua and put it in the replacement car. Believe it or not, he had another minor accident in that car as well! I guess that the reason for the problems was that the Ba Gua was not always facing forward. As it was hanging on its string it was twisting around, sometimes facing forward and sometimes backward, hence the occasional negative energy. I advised him to remove it altogether.

Other Aggressive Techniques

One of the most aggressive techniques of protection is to point a cannon at the offending structure. It is said to be more potent if the cannon has been fired in anger during some conflict or other. I came across these two cannons in Singapore in a residential garden. They would have an extremely negative effect on the opposite property.

As it turned out, they were in response to a property that had a pointed roofline and a construction crane—which was only temporary, of course. Needless to say, please do not use cannons and if you find one pointing at your property ask your neighbor to remove it or hide it with foliage or a fence.

Crossed swords are another aggressive symbol that causes harm to the opposite building. In fact, any cross shape can be harmful. There was a famous example of an office building in Kuala Lumpur that had a glass front and two rather conspicuous escalators inside that made a huge "X" shape. The office building opposite promptly installed a cannon to counteract it.

The Power of the Octagon

While the Ba Gua (and in particular the Ba Gua mirror) is very aggressive, the octagonal shape has protective properties. As I have traveled around the world I have taken an interest in the use of the octagon in various places. You often see stop signs on an octagonal background. In Singapore, the stickers that everyone must display on the windshield of their car to indicate that they have paid their car taxes are octagonal. The reason for this is quite interesting. Apparently, a bridge was built that disturbed three Form School "dragons" that have their heads there. Reverend Hong Choon is said to have advised the government to have everyone display an octagonal shape to help counteract this. Initially, new one-dollar coins were minted, featuring an octagon in the design, but since the coins were in people's pockets most of the time they therefore were not openly displayed. So it was decided to make the car tax sticker octagonal as well. Apparently this has cured the problem.

The most intriguing use of the octagon I have seen is in Florence. At the heart of this wonderful old city is the Duomo cathedral, so named because of its famous octagonal dome, the first to be constructed in Europe. You can see the red dome peeking over the top of the buildings in this picture, behind another another octagonal building: the Baptistry, with its famous "Doors of Paradise." This is said to be the oldest building in Florence.

Just inside the front door of the cathedral is another octagon, a most amazing design that looks for all the world like a European Ba Gua. What inspired this pattern? Apparently, the eight sides of the octagon represent the "eighth day of the risen Christ," hence its popularity in Florence.

There are few who would argue that Florence is the best-preserved Renaissance city in Europe, remarkable for having survived intact after so many wars and natural disasters. It appears that the octagon shape on its own (without the trigrams of the Ba Gua) has protective properties—one might even say *preservative* properties. So if you build a house or office, this floor plan is great for protection but may not be conducive to growth and development; things may tend to be preserved as they are in the beginning, and growth may be slow.

DIRECTIONS AND LOCATIONS

As I mentioned earlier, the Form School recommends that the best direction for the front door to face is south. There are good reasons for this orientation in Flying Star geomancy also. However, if you are in the west group of the Compass School, this orientation is not auspicious. Using your gua number, which you should have worked out in chapter 2, and the table opposite, you can check whether your front door faces an auspicious direction. Use a reliable compass to take the direction of the front door from the inside looking out.

The best location for the front door is in the middle of the side of the building that faces the road or the most yang feature. For instance, if your house faces a lake, or one side of the building is much brighter than the other, that is where the main door should be. You don't want your front door located at the side of the building if it faces another building, wall, or fence, as then the energy has difficulty in finding the entrance.

Gua Number	Front Door Direction	Effect
1	S	Excellent relationship luck. Easy to find a partner. Harmonious family.
	N	Easy to study and pass examinations. Possible spiritual growth. Good direction for children with a gua number of one.
2	NE	Excellent wealth luck.
	SW	Easy to study and pass examinations. Possible spiritual growth. Good direction for children with a gua number of two.
3	S	Excellent wealth luck.
	N	Excellent health and good wealth luck.
4	N	Excellent wealth luck.
	S	Excellent health and good wealth luck.
5 (Male)	NE	Excellent wealth luck.
	SW	Easy to study and pass examinations. Possible spiritual growth. Good direction for male children with a gua number of five.
5 (Female)	SW	Excellent wealth luck.
	NE	Easy to study and pass examinations. Possible spiritual growth. Good direction for female children with a gua number of five.
6	NE	Excellent health and good wealth luck.
	SW	Excellent relationship luck. Easy to find a partner. Harmonious family.
7	SW	Excellent health and good wealth luck.
	NE	Excellent relationship luck. Easy to find a partner. Harmonious family.
8	SW	Excellent wealth luck.
	NE	Easy to study and pass examinations. Possible spiritual growth. Good direction for children with a gua number of eight.
9	N	Excellent relationship luck. Easy to find a partner. Harmonious family.
	S	Easy to study and pass examinations. Possible spiritual growth. Good direction for children with a gua number of nine.

Porch

It is good to have a bright porch or portico in front of the front door. It should be brightly lit at night. This encourages the energy to collect and settle before it enters the building. The light can be above and in front of the door or you can have lights on either side. It is good if the porch is quite large, not just covering the doorway. However, be careful that it does not extend so far that it creates missing corners, like the ones discussed in chapter 4. Also make sure that the porch is not supported by many pillars that give the impression of prison bars.

Foyer

Similarly, the building should have a bright foyer, lobby, or hall where the positive energy can collect before it disperses to the various parts of the building. This should also have a bright light above and fairly close to the door. Crystal chandeliers are particularly good if they fit with your décor. Otherwise any bright light will do.

In general it is good if the front opens into a large space. You do not need to have a separate door from the lobby area to the living area. If there are no windows in the foyer, it is better to keep the light on at all times. If the foyer is too cramped, as is sometimes the case in apartments, you can make it bigger by installing mirrors on the walls to each side. But do not put one on the wall in front of the door as all that hard-earned positive energy gets reflected straight out again!

Negative Features inside the Front Door

As you look inside the front door, what can you see? As mentioned before, if there is a pillar outside the building that is directly in line with the front door, this is a poison arrow—likewise if there is one inside and in line with the front door. I had this problem with my house in India. I covered the pillar with a

Tibetan ceremonial scarf. Any kind of cloth covering or a tall bushy plant will do, as long as the pillar is hidden.

It is also a problem if there is a flight of stairs leading directly away from the front door, or inside leading straight down to the front door. If you can, angle the last few steps so that they do not face the front door; otherwise, put a screen between the stairs and the front door. In this picture you can see the problem of stairs leading down to the front door and also running down and away from it. Unfortunately, this is very common in apartment buildings.

If there is a corner facing the door, inside or outside, hide it with a tall plant in the same way as a pillar.

Bathrooms are always a problem in geomancy. If you can see a bathroom door opposite your front door, keep it closed and cover it with a heavy curtain. Do not use this bathroom if possible. It is also inauspicious if there is a bathroom located directly above the front door. Again, use an alternative bathroom if possible.

If you can directly see a window, this will allow the positive energy to zoom straight through the building without leaving any benefit. Keep the window closed and covered with a thick curtain. The same is true if you can see a back door. Put a screen in between the front and back doors to make the energy slow down and wander. You should not be able to see open shelves, sinks, or a stove.

Other things that are considered negative include mops and brushes, rubbish bins, the corner of a table, or a television. You should never have symbols of aggressive protection inside, especially opposite the front door. Avoid swords, guns, and cross shapes. Never, ever have a Ba Gua mirror inside the building.

Again, the seriousness of a poison arrow depends on how close it is. If it is an obvious feature as you look in through the door then you should try to do something to disguise or deflect it as explained before. A well-located front door causes the energy to wander—not to go in straight lines.

THE DOOR ITSELF

Door Shape

These door shapes are all fine but those on the left and the right send poison arrows to any buildings that are opposite them. Additionally, the door on the right is not as good because it opens outward rather than inward.

You should beware of fanlight windows above the door as many of these contain downward-pointing arrow shapes in the design.

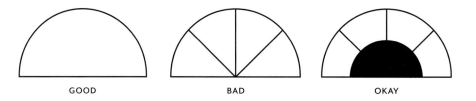

GOOD   BAD   OKAY

Door Size and Materials

The door should not be too large, nor too small; you should not need to duck your head to get in. In fact it should be the largest door in the house, but still in proportion to the rest of the building. It can be made up of a double door split down the middle. If so, it is better if one of the doors is smaller than the other. Sometimes buildings and apartments have this kind of front door so that it is easier to move furniture in and out.

The front door should be made of solid wood and have no glass panels, which offer no protection. Sliding doors (usually glass) are not so good for a front door. Having said that, I had a small house, actually just one room, that had a sliding glass door and it was perfectly okay. However, it was in quite a yin location, with a lot of foliage in front of and above the door. In a brighter, more yang place, the energy would probably come and go too quickly through such a door.

The color of the door is important. If it faces a yin place, such as a cemetery, hospital, or rubbish dump, it should be a bright, yang color such as red. The color should also be according to the recommendations given in the table of the trigrams and the cycles of the elements. The table below summarizes these.

Sector	Best Colors	Secondary Colors	Negative Colors
North	Black/blue	White/metallic	Yellow/beige/ocher
Northeast	Yellow/beige/ocher	Red/orange	Green/brown
East	Green/brown	Black/blue	White/metallic
Southeast	Light green	Light blue	White/grey
South	Red/orange	Green	Black/blue/ocher
Southwest	Yellow/beige/ocher	Red/orange	Green/brown
West	White/grey	Yellow/ocher	Red/orange/blue
Northwest	White/metallic	Yellow/ocher	Red/orange/blue

For example, if the door faces south it is good if it is red or green, and black or blue would not be good.

FRONT DOOR ORIENTATION AND THE FLOOR PLAN

Now we need to look at the front door direction and its relationship to the floor plan. It is important to have a reasonably accurate plan of the building. When I am doing a consultation and there is none available, I pace out the dimensions of the floor area and that is usually accurate enough to show if there are missing corners or not.

The extent of the floor plan is defined by the extent of the roof. You must take into account all the areas that are covered by the roof, including attached garages, carports, and verandas. These may only have fairly flimsy corrugated plastic sheeting as a roofing material but if they are adjoined to the main building they must be included in the floor plan.

Once you have an accurate idea of the shape of the floor plan, you need to take a precise compass reading on the front door. If necessary, you should review the section in chapter 2 on checking the door direction. According to the Compass School, you take the orientation of the front door to be the orientation of the building as a whole.

When you have determined the orientation of the building, you can apply the Lo Shu square to the floor plan of the building, as you did for the land as a whole. This can be quite confusing, so I will give as many examples as possible.

Applying the Lo Shu Square to the Floor Plan of the Building

The ideal shape for the floor plan is the same as for the land—a regular rectangle or square. If this is the case there is no problem with missing corners and the Lo Shu square can be very easily applied. However, this is not often the case in reality because architects find this very boring.

In example A, the building is a regular shape and the front door is located in the middle at the front facing south. It is considered better if the building is longer at the side than in the front; this gives it more depth, which is better for the flow of the positive energy. So the building in this example would not be so good because it is wider at the front than at the sides.

Now, what happens if the door faces south but is located in the southeast? (Example B.) The *orientation* of the building is still south but the front door is *located* in the southeastern quadrant rather than the southern one.

SOUTHEAST	SOUTH	SOUTHWEST
EAST	CENTER	WEST
NORTHEAST	NORTH	NORTHWEST

A

SOUTHEAST	SOUTH	SOUTHWEST
EAST	CENTER	WEST
NORTHEAST	NORTH	NORTHWEST

B

If the building faces northeast, for example, you simply reorient the quadrants as shown. (Example C.)

In example D, the front door is located in the east and faces south, so the orientation of the building is south. This building has a missing corner in the southeast.

NORTH	NORTHEAST	EAST
NORTHWEST	CENTER	SOUTHEAST
WEST	SOUTHWEST	SOUTH

C

SOUTHEAST	SOUTH	SOUTHWEST
EAST	CENTER	WEST
NORTHEAST	NORTH	NORTHWEST

D

What if the door is located at the side of the building, rather than at the front facing the road? In example E, the front door is facing west and is located in the southwest sector. This would actually be better for a west-group person than a door facing south. Though if you have a front door at the side of the house, you must make sure that there is a very well-defined path leading to it. Line it with shrubs and lights to lead the positive energy to the door.

What if the front door is at an angle? In example F, the front door has been angled to the east to suit an east-group person. The general orientation of the building is still northeast/southwest however, making it a west-group house.

SOUTHEAST	SOUTH	SOUTHWEST
EAST	CENTER	WEST
NORTHEAST	NORTH	NORTHWEST

E

NORTH	NORTHEAST	EAST
NORTHWEST	CENTER	SOUTHEAST
WEST	SOUTHWEST	SOUTH

F

Sometimes a building has a protruding corner. If the corner protrudes less than one third of the length or width of the building it does not create missing corners in other sectors. In example G, wealth luck, which is associated with the southeast, would be enhanced.

In example H, the area in the southwest protrudes so far that it makes missing corners in the south and the southeast.

Irregularly shaped buildings pose something of a problem. Which parts are protruding, which parts are missing? You just have to make your best guess and then see how it works out. In example I, the southwest, northwest, and southeast corners are almost completely missing.

Some geomancers prefer to use the compass rose to determine the various sectors in awkwardly shaped buildings (example J). You can try using both

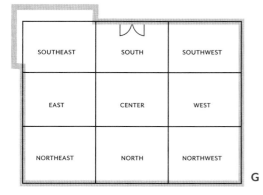

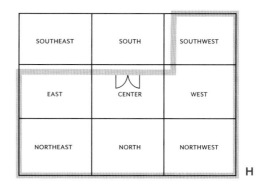

G

H

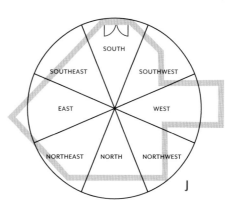

I

J

methods to determine the positions of the sectors and see where the two results coincide. Those would then be good places to locate the enhancing elements.

In chapter 4, I explained the effect of missing and protruding corners of the land as a whole. The same principles apply to the building. If a sector is missing when you apply the Lo Shu square to the floor plan, the luck associated with it is adversely affected. If there is a protruding sector, the luck is enhanced. So you must be extremely careful when planning an extension to your home and make sure that you do not make it so large that it creates missing corners. The table on the next page summarizes the types of luck influenced by each sector.

SE Wealth	**S** Reputation	**SW** Relationships
E Health	**Center** Support	**W** Children
NE Knowledge	**N** Career	**NW** Mentors

SOUTHEAST	SOUTH	SOUTHWEST
EAST	CENTER	WEST
NORTHEAST	NORTH	NORTHWEST

K

SOUTHEAST	SOUTH	SOUTHWEST
EAST	CENTER	WEST
NORTHEAST	NORTH	NORTHWEST

L

If a sector is missing, how do you compensate for it? In example K, the southeast corner is missing, so wealth luck would be adversely affected. To correct missing corners, regardless of what sector they are in, you must try to complete the regular rectangular or square shape. The materials that you would use to do this vary depending on the sector that is missing. In this case, wood is a beneficial element for the southeast, so you should put a five-foot-high wooden fence or hedge in place to complete the rectangle. At the very least you should place a tree or large shrub at the corner, in line with the two walls of the building.

If the southwest corner is missing (example L), put a bright light on a five-foot-high plastic or stonework pole. You can also complete the corner with a brick wall. At least make sure you have the light, and keep it on at least eight hours a day. This will definitely improve relationship luck.

In general, use the following materials to complete the respective missing corners:

▸ Use wood in the south, southeast, and east
▸ Use a lamp and brick or concrete in the southwest and northeast
▸ Use metal in the west, northwest, and north

If the central sector is missing—for instance if the building has a large central courtyard—put a large square-shaped structure such as a roofed pavilion in the middle. You can also put five large boulders there. Keep it brightly lit. Many European monasteries have a large open space at the center, which usually has a garden or fountain. The wood element of a garden is not compatible with the earth element, which would enhance the center of the building, and water is too changeable to provide the support needed in the center of the building. No wonder the monastic tradition has dwindled in the West.

If the building is U-shaped, as in example M, you must put a wall or fence across to complete the rectangle. Again, this fence should be at least five feet tall. Many European palaces were built on this kind of floor plan and many of the noble families lost all their power and influence; these buildings simply do not have enough support at the center.

Apartments are more difficult to correct if there are missing corners. Often apartment buildings are an irregular shape and it is almost impossible to get all the residents to agree to a major change to the building. There is one thing you can do *inside* the apartment to compensate for a missing corner and that is to use mirrors to create what is called "virtual space." If you put mirrors on the walls where the missing corner is,

M

N

you create the illusion that the sector exists *within* the mirror. This seems to be enough to compensate for the missing corner and improve the luck associated with that sector. In example N, you could put plants in front of the mirrors and the reflection would make it look as though there were plants in the southeast sector, thereby enhancing wealth luck.

In the next chapter, on interior geomancy, we will look at the specific effects of missing and protruding corners as well as the enhancing and debilitating elements for each sector.

6

Interior Geomancy

 THIS CHAPTER DEALS with the recommendations of both the Form School and the Compass School with regard to the interior of the building. First let us look at some general Form School recommendations.

INTERIOR LAYOUT

Inner Half and Outer Half

Ideally it is better if a house has more depth than width. The outer half—the half nearer the front door—should contain the areas where visitors are greeted and entertained. The kitchen, bedroom, and other private rooms should be located in the inner, or back, half of the house, though it is okay to have bedrooms located in the outer half of the house on the upper floors.

The outer half can have an open plan, especially if the front door faces an auspicious direction according to the Flying Star School. The dining room should be in the center—not too far forward or back, or too close to the front door. The kitchen and particularly toilets are a problem wherever they are located. In the old days the toilet was always well away from the main building.

Room Shape

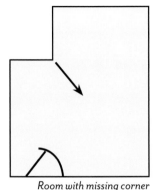

Room with missing corner

Not surprisingly, the best shape for any room is a regular square or a rectangle. A bad shape for a room is a wedge.

A protruding corner inside a room gives a poison arrow. You can put a tall plant in front of it to hide it. Fake plants are good and work just as well as real ones.

Sometimes a room has pillars in all four corners that give poison arrows all around. These are just as bad as protruding corners. One way of handling these is to square off the edges of the pillars so that you do not leave any sharp corners—actually, some geomancers recommend rounding all the corners in a room, even if they don't protrude. Alternatively, you can cover the corners or pillars with mirrors, which symbolically makes them disappear. Another option is to wall off the corners or pillars diagonally to make a Ba Gua shape. You can also construct a closet to hide a protruding corner inside.

Interior pillars in the room are also not good. In the main temple of my monastery they have intuitively covered all the pillars with brocade hangings on both the front and the back.

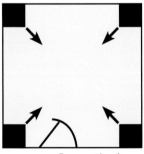

Room with columns

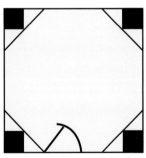

Room with Ba Gua

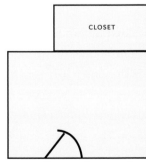

Room with corner closet

Windows

In any one room the ratio of windows to doors should not exceed three to one, and there should be at least one solid wall in the room. Windows should not be located opposite doors—otherwise the beneficial energy tends to enter the room and exit straightaway through the window. Close off any inauspicious views, such as a view of a cemetery, with curtains.

I am not fond of Venetian-style blinds; they give off poison arrows when they are open. Vertical blinds have a similar problem, although not quite so bad. Ordinary curtains and roller blinds are the best. Do not allow trees to grow too close to the windows so that they block off the view and the light.

Ceiling

Overhead beams in the ceiling are not good. Some houses in England, South Africa, and Tuscany make a feature out of this. A guesthouse I stayed at in South Africa had exposed beams in all the rooms. I didn't have the heart to tell them that they were being hit by poison arrows everywhere!

It is not good to sleep under beams like those shown here. The cross-shaped fan is also a problem—in general, sleeping or working under a ceiling fan is never recommended, but fans with four blades are particularly bad. One way to solve this would be to have a four-poster bed with a canopy between you and the beams and fan.

Even beams that are hidden behind a false ceiling are a problem, especially if they are large heavy ones. Do not sleep or sit directly under them.

Beams leading directly to a door are not good; they pollute the energy as it comes into the room. Definitely

do not have one over the front door, like the one in this picture. This room also has a sloping ceiling, which is not good.

A ceiling should never slope from one side of the room to the other, especially if it is fairly low. If it does, you need to put a lamp that shines upward at the lower end of the slope. This symbolically lifts the lower side of the ceiling.

Decorative ceiling cornices with sharp edges give off poison arrows. It is better if they have rounded shapes. The arch over the door in the picture here is good.

Hallways

A hallway should not lead in a straight line from the front door directly to the back door or a window. If it does, there is nothing to stop the energy from passing straight through the building with no beneficial effect. You must put one or two screens or big plants on either side and in between to make the energy slow down and wander. Archways also help to guide the beneficial energy through entrances and corridors.

The doors to each side of a hallway should not be opposite each other. This is called a "centipede configuration" and causes disagreements among the building's inhabitants. This centipede configuration is very common for the layout of workstations in offices. You can try putting a picture of a rooster in the hallway to counteract the centipede.

If there is a room at the end of a corridor, it receives a poison arrow from the corridor itself. So it is better not to occupy an office or bedroom at the end of a hallway.

Stairs

As I mentioned earlier, staircases should not run down directly to the front door; all the positive energy runs straight out. You can fix this problem by angling the last three or four steps so that they no longer lead straight to the door.

It is similarly not good to have the door to an upstairs room directly in line with the top of the stairs. It is especially important to avoid having the door to a bathroom in line with the top or bottom of the stairs. Also, do not have a mirror facing the stairs at the top or bottom.

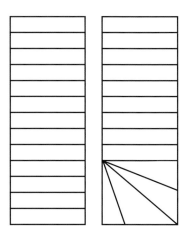

A spiral staircase is the worst type to have. Wherever it is located, it is like a corkscrew drilling down into the luck of that sector. I came across a case recently where there was a spiral staircase located in the northwest of an apartment, which is associated with the luck of the patriarch and mentors. In this case, the father of the family had had six different jobs in five years, with inexplicable bad luck in each one. In one of the jobs, the company suddenly went out of business before he could join them. Needless to say this run of bad fortune was putting great strain on his marriage as well. Spiral staircases are also a condition for mental health problems, including addiction or obsessive behavior. Often, the family member affected depends on the location of the offending staircase in the Lo Shu square applied to the building. For example, if the staircase is in the east sector, it would affect the eldest son; in a business this would be the oldest male employee.

Unfortunately there is not much you can do to fix the problem of a spiral staircase other than replace it with conventional stairs. This is usually a very expensive option, so most people just try to enhance the other sectors as much as possible. My main advice is to avoid the problem by never choosing a house or apartment with a spiral staircase.

The spiral staircase in the photograph above has another problem: the lack of proper backing for each step. This is also a problem for normal, straight staircases. Each step should be connected to the next with proper backing. You should not be able to see daylight between each step; otherwise they become like blades, giving off negative energy.

Shelves

Exposed shelving also gives off poison arrows and you should avoid sleeping or sitting for long periods in front of it. Shelves are better covered with solid doors or a curtain. One of the best solutions I have seen is to cover them with a roller blind.

Shrines

It is good to have a shrine or altar opposite the front door or the door to the family room. This attracts positive energy into the house and prevents negative energy from entering. It need not be very big; it could be just one statue or picture. You should not have a shrine opposite a bathroom or kitchen or in a bedroom. If it is in a bedroom, have it in a cupboard that can be closed and do not sleep with your feet toward it. Try to keep holy images high off the ground. Often you see Buddha images in the garden or outside a door on the ground. Keep them high off the ground and make fresh offerings of flowers to them when you can. They represent the highest state of being so we must show respect; they should not be treated like protectors. If you have a separate meditation room it should be a fairly yin place, but not completely so; use subdued lighting and earth colors, but also include a little red or orange.

Bedroom Allocation

The table of the trigrams in chapter 1 shows that each sector of the house is associated with a different family member. If that sector is missing, then the corresponding family member is adversely affected. If there is a protruding corner in the sector, then they are beneficially affected. It is good if family members' bedrooms are located in the appropriate sectors unless that is a bad Compass School direction for them, though the northwest is a good location for the master bedroom or the father's study even if he is in the east group. It should not be used for a guestroom or storeroom, and definitely should not be used for the kitchen or bathroom. The matriarch's room is best in the southwest and this can be the master bedroom if she is the chief earner.

SE Eldest daughter	S Middle daughter	SW Matriarch
E Eldest son	Center	W Youngest daughter
NE Youngest son	N Middle son	NW Patriarch

USING THE ELEMENTS INSIDE THE BUILDING

The principles for the placement of the elements in the interior of a building and for individual rooms are the same as for the land as a whole, which I explained in chapter 4. They apply equally to houses, apartments, shops, and offices. No matter what the size of the space, you can use the Lo Shu square to see what type of luck is influenced in each sector, and begin to enhance that luck with the presence of one of the five elements: water, wood, fire, earth, or metal. I have already explained the effect of each element on each of the nine types of luck in detail in chapter 4, which you can refer back to; the same principles apply inside the building as outside, but the elements are used a little differently.

Water, for instance, can be represented inside the building by a fish tank, small water fountain, pictures of water of various kinds, or a water-storage tank. It is often recommended that a fish tank should have eight gold fish and one black fish for wealth luck. Water features should generally be moving and must be kept clean. Make sure the flow in any water feature is toward the center of the building; this represents wealth coming in. Sometimes a master geomancer will recommend keeping still water but that is only to control a negative Flying Star influence. The water in toilets and bathrooms is polluted and not considered beneficial. Wavy shapes are associated with water, as well as the colors black and blue. Blue flowers and other blue-colored objects are good. One place where you cannot have water is in the bedroom. This is because water is considered a yang feature and bedrooms should be more yin and hence restful. A water tank above the bedroom is also bad, especially if it is directly above the bed.

There are two types of wood in the table of the trigrams: big and small. Small wood is represented by flowers, small plants, and small wooden objects, and by the color light green. Do not use dried flowers or potpourri—they are dead. Bonsai trees represent stunted growth and will not work. Cacti give off poison arrows from all the spikes and should not be kept inside the building. Succulents are good. Big wood is represented by heavy wooden furniture such as tables, cupboards, dressers, and wardrobes, and by darker green and rectangular shapes. As there is so much wood throughout most houses, including in the structure of the house, you must try to make sure that unnecessary wooden objects are kept from those areas where they are detrimental: the southwest, center, north, and northeast.

Fire can be represented by lamps, candles, stoves, ovens, heaters, and fireplaces. The shape associated with the fire element is the triangle, though you must be careful not to use triangular-shaped objects that make poison arrows. The color of the fire element is red, and it is good to use red flowers. Stoves and ovens are generally considered to burn up the luck of the area where they are located.

There are two types of earth element: big earth and small earth. Big earth is represented by stone flooring, statues, and large ceramic vases. Small earth is represented by small ceramic figures, crystals, and semi-precious stones. They are both associated with the square shape and earth colors: ocher, terracotta, sand, and so on.

There are also two types of metal: big and small. Big metal is represented by heavy metal objects such as a safe or large metal cabinet as well as large wind chimes; small metal by smaller wind chimes, bells, and trophies. The colors associated with metal are white and metallic. The shape associated with metal is the circle. Wind chimes can be used inside the building; it does not matter if they make a sound or not for them to work.

The Elements by Sector

The main enhancing element, the productive and supportive elements, and the two elements that must be avoided are the same for each sector inside the building as they are outside (see the table on the next page).

You can use large amounts of the enhancing element in each sector. You can also use large amounts of the element from the productive cycle, but you should not use large amounts of the element from the supportive cycle. You should avoid the destructive- and exhaustive-cycle elements altogether or at least keep them to a minimum.

On page 109 is the table of colors that correspond to the sectors, arranged by sector. Use this table to decorate your building with the most auspicious colors. For instance, a room in the north sector could have blue walls, with white trim around the windows, and should not have any green, yellow, beige, or ocher.

SE **Wealth**	S **Reputation**	SW **Relationships**
Enhanced by small wood *Produced by* water *Supported by* small earth *Destroyed by* metal *Exhausted by* fire	*Enhanced by* fire *Produced by* wood *Supported by* small metal *Destroyed by* water *Exhausted by* earth	*Enhanced by* big earth *Produced by* fire *Supported by* small water *Destroyed by* wood *Exhausted by* metal
E **Health**	Center **Support**	W **Children**
Enhanced by big wood *Produced by* water *Supported by* small earth *Destroyed by* metal *Exhausted by* fire	*Enhanced by* earth *Produced by* fire *Supported by* small water *Destroyed by* wood *Exhausted by* metal	*Enhanced by* small metal *Produced by* earth *Supported by* small wood *Destroyed by* fire *Exhausted by* water
NE **Knowledge**	N **Career**	NW **Mentors**
Enhanced by small earth *Produced by* fire *Supported by* small water *Destroyed by* wood *Exhausted by* metal	*Enhanced by* water *Produced by* metal *Supported by* small fire *Destroyed by* earth *Exhausted by* wood	*Enhanced by* big metal *Produced by* earth *Supported by* small wood *Destroyed by* fire *Exhausted by* water

Balancing Yin and Yang Elements

You will remember that the Taoist yin/yang symbol illustrates the importance of having a proper balance of each. Yin and yang are intertwined; in the yang there must be a little yin and in the yin a little yang. This means that you must be similarly careful to balance the energies in each part of your building.

The earth element is considered more yin and the metal, wood, and fire elements more yang. Water is considered yin when it is still and yang when it is active.

Table of Colors that Correspond to the Sectors

SE	**S**	**SW**
Dominant colors: light green	*Dominant colors:* red, orange	*Dominant colors:* yellow, beige, ocher
Secondary colors: light blue	*Secondary colors:* green	*Secondary colors:* red, orange
Negative colors: white, grey	*Negative colors:* black, blue, ocher	*Negative color:* green
E	**Center**	**W**
Dominant colors: green, brown	*Dominant colors:* yellow, beige, ocher	*Dominant colors:* white, grey
Secondary colors: black, blue	*Secondary colors:* red, orange	*Secondary colors:* yellow, ocher
Negative colors: white, metallics	*Negative color:* green	*Negative colors:* red, orange, blue
NE	**N**	**NW**
Dominant colors: yellow, beige, ocher	*Dominant colors:* black, blue	*Dominant colors:* white, metallics
Secondary colors: red, orange	*Secondary colors:* white, metallics	*Secondary colors:* yellow, ocher
Negative color: green	*Negative colors:* green, yellow, beige, ocher	*Negative colors:* red, orange, blue

Yin colors are those associated with the earth and still water elements: ocher, brown, grey, tan, black, dark blue. Yang colors are those associated with the wood, fire, and metal elements: red, orange, green, white, metallics, and light blue, representing active water.

GEOMANCY FOR INDIVIDUAL ROOMS

Living Room

The living room should be located in the front half of the house or apartment. It is okay if the front door opens directly into the living room. It is also good if there is a bright lobby that leads into the living room through an archway. Archways help to channel positive energy.

If your home is split-level, make sure that the living room is lower than the dining room and the bedroom. There should be a good balance of yin and yang colors and features. Mirrors are good, especially to cure missing corners in the living room. Make sure that there is no mirror facing the front door, staircase, or bathroom. It is good to arrange the furniture in a square or octagonal shape. Avoid a U- or L-shaped layout. Make sure that you disarm all the poison arrows, especially those hitting the places where you often sit.

Put enhancing features in each corner of the living room. Put plants and flowers in the southeast, east, and south. Put ceramics in the southwest, northeast, center, west, and northwest. Put water in the north. Have an aquarium in the southeast with eight gold fish and one black fish. The television is best located in the south of the living room. The southwest and northeast are okay if the cabinet is not predominantly wood or metal. The north, west, and northwest are okay if it is only a small television.

Dining Room

The dining room should be located in the center of the house or apartment. Each family member should be able to sit facing a good direction—preferably his or her health direction.

The table should have the shape of the element of the sector in which the dining room is located: In the center, southwest, or northeast it should be square and should have a marble top. In the east, southeast, and south, it should be rectangular and made from wood. If the dining room is in the west, northwest, or northern sector of the building, the table should be metal or white and round.

All tables should have rounded edges to minimize poison arrows from the corners and edges of the table. A glass top is never recommended because it does not give solid support. Oval-shaped tables are a good compromise in all sectors.

The dining table should not be in view of the main door. Put a screen in between them if necessary. The dining area should also be separate from the kitchen. Again, use a screen to separate them if necessary. The whole area should be more yang than yin so keep it well lit, use bright colors, and have a television or stereo there. It should not be near a bathroom or located under one on the floor above. A large mirror next to the dining table is very good because it symbolically multiplies the food. It is also good to have a painting of fruit and other food.

The dining room shown here is located in the south, so it has the proper rectangular shape, and the use of the mirror and the yang colors are very good. The only problem is the glass-topped table.

Kitchen

The kitchen should be located in the inner half of the building and should be yang, so use bright colors and wood. There will always be metal and fire represented by the stove. Fire and water should not be in conflict so keep the stove, sink, and refrigerator on separate sides of the kitchen.

According to the Compass School, the stove burns away the luck of the sector in which it is located, whether good or bad. This means that if the kitchen is located in one of your inauspicious sectors the stove will help to burn up your bad luck, and if it is in one of your auspicious sectors the good luck is burned up. For instance, if you are gua one and the kitchen is located in the southwest it will burn up your "total loss" luck and you will have more success. On the other hand if it is in the east it will burn up your "health" luck and you will suffer from more sickness.

Check the table showing the gua numbers in chapter 2 to see what the effect of the kitchen is on the luck of each person in your house. When you are looking for a new house or apartment, make sure that the kitchen is not located in one of the auspicious directions of the main breadwinner.

Above all you should make sure that the kitchen is not located in the northwest sector, regardless of your gua number. This is known as "Fire at Heaven's Gate." You will remember that the trigram of the northwest is Qian—the most yang trigram. In the I Ching it represents heavenly forces. Alfred Huang says, "It possesses the attributes of initiation, prosperity, harmony, and steadfastness." Therefore it is very important to protect this sector from negative influences, especially the stove. If the kitchen is in the northwest of your property and there is nothing you can do about it, at least make sure that the stove is not in the northwest corner of the kitchen itself. Fire at Heaven's Gate is one of the major taboos in feng shui and must be avoided. It is particularly damaging for the man of the house.

Regardless of where the kitchen is located, you must make sure that the power to the stove comes from one of your good directions. In the old days, this meant that the mouth of the wood- or coal-burning stove faced one of your good directions. As I explained in chapter 2, with modern appliances this means that the socket or cable going into the stove should be coming from a good direction based on your gua number. In other words, the power should come into the appliance from one of your good directions. This is the same for the other appliances such as kettles, rice cookers, and microwave ovens.

Watch out for poison arrows in the kitchen; you do not want to be hit by negative energy while you are cooking. As I mentioned earlier, exposed shelves give negative energy wherever you find them. They are like blades cutting in to you. Cover shelves with cupboard doors, curtains, or roller blinds. Make sure that kitchen benches and tables have rounded corners.

Bathrooms

Bathrooms influence luck wherever they are located, much the way the stove does, so it is good if the bathroom is located in your "total loss" direction.

However, this may not suit everyone who lives in the house. It seems that these days everyone wants bedrooms with their own large and luxurious attached bathrooms, but the more toilets there are in a house, the more sectors will be adversely affected. It is better for everyone to share one small bathroom that has the least overall negative effect.

There are some cures for toilets in certain areas:

▸ If the toilet is in the southwest, center, or northeast sectors, use boulders to symbolically press down on the bad luck. Put a large boulder, piece of marble, or building block next to the bathroom.

▸ If the toilet is in the west, northwest, or northern sectors, hang a large metal wind chime with six hollow rods in the bathroom.

▸ If the toilet is in the southern center, hang a smaller wind chime.

There is no real cure for other areas. If possible do not use toilets in the east or southeastern sectors.

In general:

▸ You must not have a bathroom directly over the front door or dining room.

▸ Bathrooms should not be located at the top or bottom of stairs or at the end of a hallway.

▸ Keep the bathroom as small as possible.

▸ Keep the lid of the toilet down.

▸ Keep the bathroom door closed and covered with a heavy curtain.

▸ Build a low wall to separate the toilet from the rest of the bathroom.

▸ Do not have symbols of success such as awards in the bathroom.

▸ Do not have pictures of anything you aspire to.

To illustrate this last point, some friends of mine were hoping to have a child but were having difficulty. Then my friend realised that he had decorated the bathroom with pictures he had taken on their travels around the world, many of which featured children. He removed them and his wife conceived soon after.

Bedrooms

Bedrooms are some of the most important rooms in the house or apartment. The bedroom is the place where you and your family members spend up to one third of your lives, so it is important to get the geomancy right. It is good if a person's bedroom is located in one of their good Compass School directions.

Master Bedroom

The master bedroom is particularly important, as the luck of the whole family is largely dependent on that of the patriarch or matriarch. It is therefore particularly important that it be arranged well.

Do not locate the master bedroom above a garage or storeroom; these rooms lack substance and do not give a strong enough basis for the bedroom. If there are several levels in the house, the bedroom should not be on the lowest level—definitely not in the basement if there is one. Basement apartments are not considered good for this reason.

As mentioned earlier, the master bedroom should not be above the kitchen. They say that sleeping over food cooked for the family is bad. At least make sure that the bed is not directly over the stove. The bedroom door must not face the stairs. If this is the case, put a screen in between or change the angle of the top three or four steps so that they do not face the door. It is not good to have another door directly opposite the bedroom door. The bedroom door must face one of your good Compass School directions.

As usual, it is better if the room is a regular rectangle or square shape; then you can use the enhancing elements in each corner easily. The floor plan should not be wedge-shaped and the ceiling should not slope. The master bedroom should be a place of rest and relaxation, so it should be mainly yin, but with a balance of yin and yang energies. You can use earth colors and more subtle yang colors such as pink for a little yang energy. It should have a predominantly feminine feel.

Do not have plants, metal, or water, because these are all yang elements.

Likewise, have subdued, well-shaded lighting. A television or computer is also considered too yang for the master bedroom. On the other hand, do not allow it to become too yin. Make sure that you let plenty of light and fresh air into the room in the morning.

The only element that is safe for the master bedroom is earth. It is especially good to have a crystal pendant hanging in a window in the southwest of the room where it can catch the afternoon sunlight. It is also good to have a pair of porcelain ducks in the southwest of the bedroom for relationship luck.

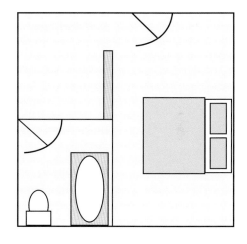

If you have an en suite bathroom like the floorplan shown here, it often creates an L-shaped bedroom. If this is the case then put a screen across the room to cut off the protruding corner and make the room a regular shape. This has the added advantage of screening off the bathroom from the bedroom and nullifying the poison arrow from the corner of the bathroom.

Make sure that you are well protected from poison arrows in general; if you are not, you can expect pains, headaches and poor sleep. I often see bedside cabinets with sharp corners that are pointing at the sleeper all night. Cover them with a cloth. Likewise, exposed shelves must be covered with doors, curtains, or a roller blind. Do not have a ceiling fan directly over the bed, and beware of cornices with sharp edges. Four-poster beds with a canopy and some curtains are actually very good for overcoming problems from poison arrows. Sadly, they are not particularly fashionable at the moment, though they are also excellent for dealing with mosquitoes if, like me, you prefer to avoid killing them.

Protruding corners are always a problem in the bedroom; try building cupboards along the wall to hide corners or other irregular shapes. You cannot cover them with plants as plants are too yang for a bedroom, and mirrors symbolically increase the number of people in the bedroom and cause problems between the partners.

Do not use mirrors to cure geomancy problems in the bedroom—for example, to cover pillars. They are likely to do more harm than good. Mirrors are good if they are inside wardrobe doors. At least make sure that the mirror does not face the bed or the door.

Bed Position

The bed position is very important. It is most important to sleep with your head toward one of your good directions. Just as you need good support behind the house as a whole, you also need to have good support behind the bed, so always try to have a solid wall behind the head of the bed. If you need to have the bed at a diagonal, due to an auspicious Compass School sleeping direction, you must have a solid headboard, but the benefit of the auspicious sleeping direction far outweighs the effect of sleeping with your head in toward a corner.

You should not have a window behind the head of the bed as this gives a lack of support. If there is no way to change it, then close the window and draw the curtains at night. Do not have the foot of the bed facing the bedroom door under any circumstances, as the bed in this diagram is doing; this is called the "death" position in both China and Italy. If your feet face an attached bathroom door, the effect is even worse. Move the bed to one side or the other to solve this problem.

If the bed is between the bedroom door and the bathroom door, like in this diagram, it receives a double

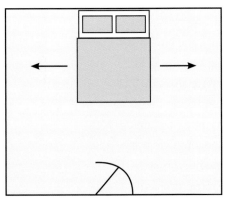

Bed in the "death" position

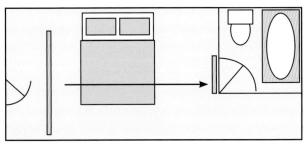

Bed between doors

FENG SHUI: SEEING IS BELIEVING

dose of negative energy. I have seen this situation in many master bedrooms. Place a screen between the bedroom door and the bed and a put a heavy curtain over the bathroom door. A heavy curtain is always good over any bathroom door in the house. Always keep bathroom doors closed and toilet lids down.

It is also bad to sleep with your feet pointing toward a window or with the bed positioned between the door and a window. Do not position the bed so that your head is toward a wall that is shared with a bathroom. And as previously mentioned, do not sleep under a bathroom on the floor above, or under beams, fans, or sharp cornices.

Do not have a water tank above any bedrooms. If the bed is under a tank, then move the bed to one side. Never put fish tanks in a bedroom. Water features do not work as geomancy enhancements in the bedroom and may well cause harm.

The first three examples here are good orientations of the bed in relation to the door. In general it is better if the bed is in the opposite corner to the door. The bed in the first example is not pointing directly at the door because it is at an angle to it, so that is okay.

The next two examples are bad orientations of the bed in relation to the door. In the first example, the head of the bed is against the wall that is shared with the door. In the other, the bed is directly opposite the door, which "cuts" into the bed as it is opened—this one is bad even if the bed is in a good Compass School direction.

Other Bedrooms

Bedrooms for the other family members should be allocated according to the Lo Shu square, but this is overridden by the personal Compass School directions. So, for instance, if the youngest daughter is in the east group, it is better not to put her in a bedroom located in the west sector of the house, even though that is where

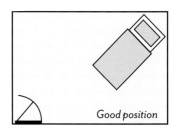

Good position

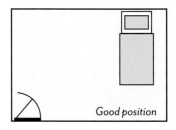

Good position

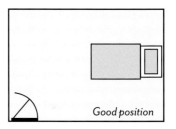

Good position

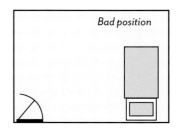

Bad position

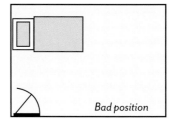

Bad position

the Lo Shu square says the youngest daughter is supposed to go. For her, any of the east group locations would be better, especially the "development" one.

Children's bedrooms should be more yang than yin because they are growing and should be full of energy; it is actually beneficial for them to have a television, stereo, computer, and so on in the bedroom. It is also good to decorate the room with bright colors. Again, this does not mean that there should be a total absence of yin energy; as always, balance is important. For instance, use yin colors for bedding. Avoid pictures of aggressive animals or symbols of war. Always keep war toys stored away.

The child's bed and desk should always be in his or her Compass School development direction. Otherwise, the arrangement of the room is the same as for an adult. Avoid having a window or door directly behind the desk or bed; they need good support behind. Beware of poison arrows, especially beams, corners of cupboards, exposed shelves, hooks, and nails. Do not have a tree growing too close to the bedroom window because it may restrict the light and hence the yang energy that the child needs. These are examples of a good arrangement of furniture for a child's bedroom:

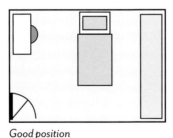

Good position

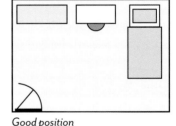

Good position

This is a bad arrangement of furniture because both the bed and the desk are between the door and the window:

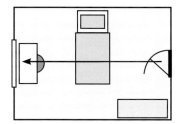

Bad position

To help your child with their studies use a compass to find the northeast of the room. Then hang a crystal pendant in the window to catch the morning light. It is also good to have a lamp with a glass shade in the northeast of the bedroom. Put a globe of the earth in the northwest for help from teachers and mentors. Put their metal trophies in the west or northwest of the room. Put wooden objects in the east and southeast for health and wealth luck, and put a metal turtle or tortoise in the north for overall support. It is better not to have water in the child's bedroom. If your child is somewhat rebellious and difficult, get them to sleep in their Compass School relationships direction and that should cure the problem.

If you have any other relatives staying with you—for instance, grandparents— follow their personal Compass School directions, and the general instructions for arranging furniture.

Storerooms

Storerooms tend to collect too much yin energy, so they will negatively affect the luck of the sector where they are located. Make sure that you air them regularly, keep them tidy, and use them often. If they contain mops and brooms, keep the doors closed at all times. In general, sell or give away anything you have not used for the last couple or years.

Clutter

Likewise, general clutter negatively affects the sector in which it is located. So, for example, if the southwest of your place has that musty smell that you get from old stuff that has not been cleaned, aired, or moved around for a long time, it attracts yin energy—and that adversely affects relationships.

Garages

In a garage, the energy is more yang. It is better if the garage is separate from the main house. Garages are considered to be empty rooms, so rooms above lack proper support.

A Word about Apartments

In general, everything I have said about houses applies equally to apartments. Sometimes geomancy is extremely difficult in them because of the excessive amount of metal that is used in modern construction; I often find extraordinary variations in the magnetic field. This makes it very difficult to decide which direction is which and therefore what elements belong where. If the magnetic field is normal then you can enhance each sector in exactly the way I have described in this chapter.

You should avoid choosing an apartment building that has missing corners, although unfortunately most do. Watch out for poison arrows hitting the front door of the building. It is not good if the apartment building has a swimming pool on the roof. Check the geomancy of the lobby, stairs, hallways, and so on.

If the front door of your apartment faces the same direction as the main door of the building, this may be good from a Flying Star point of view; if the main door is auspicious then that auspiciousness pervades the apartments that have front doors in the same direction. Regardless, the front door of the apartment building, the front door of your apartment, and your bedroom door should all face your good directions.

Apartment garages that are in underground basements are better than exposed ones on the ground floor under a building. There is a photograph of such a garage in chapter 3. If the ground floor is open like the one in that picture then the whole building lacks a proper foundation.

Office

The same principles that apply to an apartment building apply to an office building. The front door of your office building, the door to your suite of offices, and the door to your personal office should ideally all face your good personal directions. Your desk should, as well. Make sure that the jack of your telephone or fax and the cable for your email come from one of your good directions.

Make sure you have solid support behind your chair: not a window or a door. Put a picture of a mountain behind you. If you are

in an open-plan office, put a screen behind if you can. In this example, the desk does not have enough support behind and is getting hit with poison arrows from the window frames and the exposed shelf.

Put roller blinds or cupboard doors on exposed shelves. Watch out for poison arrows in general; it is better to have desks that have rounded edges. Do not sit under a beam or in front of the corner of a wall or pillar. You can use all the enhancements I have explained in this chapter—put plants in the southeast for wealth, and so on.

Try not to sit directly opposite someone else or have an office door directly opposite another one. The location of the desk within the office follows the same principles as the bed location in a bedroom. The ideal position is opposite the door and to one side, with a wall behind you.

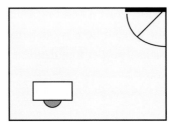

These principles apply equally to a study or office at home and can basically be used for any type of workplace.

That concludes our look at interior geomancy. Next we will briefly examine the time dimension of geomancy.

7

Geomancy over Time

NTIL NOW I have mainly been discussing the effects of topography, position, and direction on your luck. This static aspect of geomancy is very important, but the changes that take place over time are even more so. The subtle, periodic changes that take place are the field of study of the Flying Star School. Feng shui masters have developed an extremely powerful method of predicting these changes, then enhancing positive effects and minimizing negative ones.

A detailed explanation of Flying Star geomancy is beyond the scope of this book, I'm afraid; it is very complicated and requires a detailed understanding of the relationships between the elements and their trigrams. But there are simpler aspects that are very useful to know.

The main thing you should understand at this stage is that there are three negative time influences that move yearly:

- The Grand Duke
- The Five Yellows
- The Three Killings

Always remember to check the position of these according to the tables below at the beginning of each year and move your sitting direction and plan any home renovations accordingly.

GRAND DUKE

The Grand Duke is the name of a negative influence that moves around the compass by 30 degrees each year. The main advice is not to sit facing the direction of the Grand Duke—even if it is your best direction—nor do renovations in the sector where it is located for that year. If you plan major renovations to the whole building, do not start them in that sector. They say it is okay to sleep with your head toward the Grand Duke but to be on the safe side maybe it is better not to. You can sit with your back toward it, but do not face it.

The location of the Grand Duke is as follows:

Year	Compass Direction	Direction in degrees	Year	Compass Direction	Direction in degrees
2012	East-southeast	113 to 127	2019	North-northwest	323 to 337
2013	South-southeast	143 to 157	2020	Due north	353 to 7
2014	Due south	173 to 187	2021	North-northeast	23 to 37
2015	South-southwest	203 to 217	2022	East-northeast	53 to 67
2016	West-southwest	223 to 247	2023	Due east	83 to 97
2017	Due west	263 to 277	2024	East-southeast	113 to 127
2018	West-northwest	293 to 307			

THREE KILLINGS

The Three Killings is another very negative yearly influence, but unlike the Grand Duke, it only affects the cardinal directions. Also unlike the Grand Duke, which you must not face, it is important not to sit with your back to this direction, and you can face this direction with no problem. The effect of sitting with your back to this direction is that you could get stabbed in the back, so to speak. This was my experience one year. I paid no attention to the fact that I was sitting with my back toward the Three Killings and found that some people began acting very strangely toward me. I subsequently discovered that someone I thought was a friend was spreading untrue gossip about me.

Avoid doing renovations in the sector that houses the Three Killings, which is said to cause accidents, illness, and financial losses. The Three Killings always moves in a counterclockwise direction, 90 degrees at a time. The location of the Three Killings is as follows for the next few years:

Year	Compass Direction	Direction in Degrees	Year	Compass Direction	Direction in Degrees
2012	South	158 to 202	2019	West	248 to 292
2013	East	68 to 112	2020	South	158 to 202
2014	North	338 to 22	2021	East	68 to 112
2015	West	248 to 292	2022	North	338 to 22
2016	South	158 to 202	2023	West	248 to 292
2017	East	68 to 112	2024	South	158 to 202
2018	North	338 to 22			

FIVE YELLOWS

The worst of the yearly influences is called the Five Yellows. This really is deadly. If it occurs in the sector that contains your front door, it is very pernicious; it can cause sickness and all kinds of mishaps. I had a very hard year once because of this. Everyone I met that year that had the same door orientation as my house had the same kind of problems—for instance, we all had car accidents involving a collision from the rear.

Every year the Five Yellows moves into one of the nine sectors of the building, bringing a very heavy earth-element influence. Over the next few years it will influence the following sectors:

Year	Sector Location	Things Affected
2012	Southeast	Wealth; eldest daughter; hips and thighs
2013	Center	Support for the whole family or business
2014	Northwest	Help from mentors; patriarch; head and lungs
2015	West	Children, especially youngest daughter; mouth
2016	Northeast	Knowledge and exams; youngest son; hands and fingers
2017	South	Reputation and fame; middle daughter; eyes
2018	North	Career luck; middle son; ears
2019	Southwest	Relationship luck; matriarch; stomach and womb
2020	East	Health; eldest son; legs and feet
2021	Southeast	Wealth; eldest daughter; hips and thighs
2022	Center	Support for the whole family or business
2023	Northwest	Help from mentors; patriarch; head and lungs
2024	West	Children, especially youngest daughter; mouth

Notice that the Five Yellows follows a distinct pattern, which it repeats; for 2025 it would move from the west to the northeast, and then to the south the following year, and so on. This sequence of movement is a fundamental aspect of Flying Star geomancy.

To control negative Flying Star influences, it is always best to use the exhaustive cycle of the elements. Therefore to exhaust the earth influence of the Five Yellows, hang a six-rod metal wind chime in the affected sector. Six represents big metal in the table of the trigrams, so that is the best number of rods to have. The wind chime should be made of hollow tubes.

You may wonder if problems arise when the Five Yellows is in a sector where metal is destructive, such as the east and the southeast. In these sectors, you might think the metal may cause even more problems. However, it is considered more important to counter the Five Yellows than to protect the element of the sector that it is afflicting. This is even more important when the front door is in the afflicted sector. In this case, the negative energy from the Five Yellows affects the whole building so it is extremely important to apply the remedial wind chime. In my experience some negative luck always results from the Five Yellows, but it is worse without the wind chime to counteract it.

2004's Geomancy Time Bomb

As we approached the year 2004, there was a time bomb ticking away in the front doors of the majority of buildings in the world. Most of us were completely unaware of the danger and naturally assumed that whatever luck we had enjoyed in the past twenty years would continue thereafter. The truth was that we were actually heading for difficult and dangerous times.

Flying Star geomancy has sixty-year, twenty-year, yearly, monthly, and daily cycles. From 1984 to 2004 we were in a period where the number seven was dominant. This is normally an unlucky number according to the Flying Star School, but in that twenty-year-long period seven became lucky. The majority of houses, apartments, and business premises are now period-seven buildings because they were either built after 1984 or had major renovations up to 2004.

In 2004, we moved into period eight. Eight is a very lucky number—even more so in this period—but seven reverted to its old pernicious connotation of violence and robbery. This means that all those period-seven buildings, after enjoying twenty years of good luck, became very unlucky *overnight*. In fact we saw an increase in violence in the world as the period of seven came to a close. This period change was much more dangerous than those that took place in 1964 or 1984.

Geomancers warned many Chinese communities around the world of this danger, who booked builders and decorators for the week following the Chinese New Year in 2004—so that the buildings could be symbolically reborn into the new period, thereby becoming period-eight buildings instead of period seven. Some buildings have particular conditions that meant they updated themselves automatically, but others needed to be deliberately changed. This can be done by basically making some changes to the front door and exposing the roof for a few days. If you started to have problems in February 2004, and they are continuing to arrive, you need to update your building. Once your building is in period eight and the front door is oriented to an auspicious direction, it will become extremely fortunate; the danger from period seven will disappear immediately.

The Flying Star School of geomancy is a lifetime of study and practice in itself, and is extremely important because its recommendations can override the Compass School in the same way that the Compass School can override the Form School. The front door direction is crucial in Flying Star geomancy and you need specific knowledge to be able to make the necessary changes successfully. These major changes will be the focus of my next book. I do not mean to scare you—for the moment just bear in mind that you may need to consult a geomancer or do some research into Flying Star if you want to avoid the problems that may have arisen from 2004 onward.

That is just a glimpse of the intricacies of Flying Star geomancy and I hope it inspires you to take your knowledge to the next level.

8

Solving Problems with Geomancy

I HAVE GIVEN YOU a lot of information—too much to be digested easily, I know. It will take most of you at least a year of experimentation to start to get the hang of it. In fact, I do not advise you to even try to implement all the possible enhancements at once. Instead, start small. Houses that have *all* the geomancy recommendations in place are very highly energized and it takes a similarly strong personality to be able to ride the extremely vibrant atmosphere that is generated. I recently spent a few days at a friend's house putting everything possible into effect at his request, and he is amazed at the resulting changes to his life. Not only has his material fortune changed but his outlook on life is also undergoing a fundamental shift. So beware!

It is much better to implement changes slowly, putting in one enhancement at a time. The knowledge you have so far is enough to cover most of your problems, but there are specific circumstances that arise in Flying Star geomancy that override the Compass and Form School recommendations and may make some of them detrimental. If you apply many changes at once you may not know which one is causing a problem. You should be especially careful with the placement of water features, crystals, and wind chimes.

If you apply one enhancement and see a beneficial result, you will have more faith in geomancy. Then you can move on to the next one with more confidence. It is much better to deal with one problem at a time—for instance if you have specific career problems—and implement those recommendations first. As the proverb says, "Make haste slowly."

With this in mind, and as a way of showing you how to put all the information I have given you together, I have summarized all the recommendations for each type of luck into checklists. Unless you are truly desperate to solve a problem area, please go through the lists one point at a time, taking a few days to check the result of each. If your luck has been negatively affected, then you can easily identify and remove the "enhancement." This is the safest approach.

SOLVING WEALTH PROBLEMS

I will start by summarizing the wealth recommendations, as this is what most people seem to most want! Money cannot bring you happiness but you need to have plenty of it before you can learn that lesson, I suppose. Wealth is the easiest to achieve with geomancy. There are more formulas and methods concerned with wealth than for anything else. Remember—apply one tip at a time. Do not go overboard!

▶ Protect your home and workplace from poison arrows—this tip applies to all types of problems.

▶ If the main door is seriously afflicted, close it and use another one as the main door, but check the direction of the new door and get someone to check the Flying Star geomancy of it if possible.

▶ If the main door leads to the garage, use the road/house orientation to determine the wealth direction. This is usually also the direction of the most yang energy. See if there is a door in that sector that could be used as the main door. If the wealth direction is not possible then use a door facing the health, relationships, or development direction. Think of this secondary door as your main door and always use it. This seems to work.

▶ Energize the southeast with small wood, light green colors, and rectangular shapes supported by the water element: wavy shapes and blue or black colors. Use green plants; even fake silk ones work but keep them clean.

- Do not use dried, dead plants or potpourri. Dried desert flowers are popular in Australia because they give off a nice fragrance, but it is better not to have them in the house; they are too yin. Bonsai trees are stunted and no good.

- Cacti are no good inside; outside they give protection.

- Correct a missing southeast corner of the house with a hedge or line of tallish shrubs.

- You can also correct a missing corner inside the house or apartment by putting a mirror on the wall where the missing corner is to create "virtual" space, but make sure it does not reflect the main door, kitchen, or bathroom.

- Fish symbolise richness and abundance, so have a bubbling aquarium in the southeast of your living room. Keep eight gold fish and one black fish.

- Carp are very lucky fish and the *lo han* or flowerhorn fish, pictured here, is the most auspicious fish for our current period, and is said to help with wealth. They are very inquisitive fish and look like they have large brains. They can grow quite large so bear that in mind if you get a small one.

- Hang a multifaceted crystal in the southeast window. The resulting rainbows in the morning are laden with heaven's breath.

- Keep a turtle, live or metal, in the north. One is enough.

- Water features should always flow toward the center of the house or apartment to symbolize wealth coming in.

- Rivers and roads should flow in a way that brings prosperity. For north, south, east, and west orientations, this is from left to right. For northeast, southeast, southwest, and northwest orientations, this is from right to left.

- Do not have the stove in the northwest of the house or the northwest of the kitchen. This is called "Fire at Heaven's Gate" and is very bad for wealth.

- Water on the left side of the door (as you are looking out) is good for wealth.

- Make sure you use the wealth directions for all important locations and activities:
  - The front door
  - Sleeping
  - Eating
  - Cooking
  - The bedroom door
  - The office door
  - Working direction
  - Phone/fax/email line
  - Sitting in general
  - Meetings and negotiations
  - Travel

- Do not sit, sleep, eat, or work under a bathroom or a beam.

- Do not have the front door under a bathroom.

- Do not use a bathroom in the southeast; there is no cure for the effect this will have on your luck.

- Do not have metal in the southeast.

- Do not sit in front of exposed shelves. Cover them with a roller blind.

- Always have a solid wall behind your bed and your workplace.

- Beware of protruding corners.

- Do not have your bed against a wall that is shared with a bathroom.

- If you have a shop, put the cash register at the back, not near the door.

- Use the lucky number eight in your phone number, address, business cards, and so on; eight is the lucky number until 2024, so using eight represents current prosperity.

- Avoid the Five Yellows, the Three Killings, and the Grand Duke.

- Use productive elements and avoid exhaustive and destructive ones. Water is productive for wealth in the southeast corner of the garden, the house, and the living room.

- Fire is exhaustive so avoid excessive light, red colors, triangular shapes, and representations of a phoenix in the southeast.

- Metal is destructive so avoid metal objects, white colors, round shapes, and representations of a tiger in the southeast.

- Finally remember that, from a Buddhist point of view, the cause of wealth is generosity. So create a flow of wealth in and out. You must make room for more to come in!

SOLVING ROMANCE AND RELATIONSHIP PROBLEMS

- Activate relationship luck with the big earth element in the southwest. Use crystals, ceramics, square shapes, and ocher colors.

- Support the fire element with lights, red colors, and triangular shapes.

- Avoid metal, white, and round shapes.

- Wood is destructive. Do not have plants, wood, green colors, or rectangular shapes in the southwest.

- Don't forget that you can enhance the southwest in the garden, the whole house, living room, and bedroom.

- It is okay to have a little water in the southwest, but not too much.

- Light and crystals together are very good. A chandelier in the southwest is one of the best ways to energise the sector.

- Put a picture of a mountain in the southwest to symbolize big earth.

- Do not use plants to cure protruding corners inside a room in the southwest.

- Cure an external missing corner with a bright light and a boulder. Inside, use a mirror to create "virtual" space as explained before.

- A red wall in the southwest will quickly start romance.

- Hang a crystal in the southwest to catch the afternoon light.

- Create a balance of yang and yin in the southwest.

- Don't send red roses unless you remove the thorns.

- Women who wish to attract potential husbands should make sure there is sufficient yang energy in the home—men who are looking for wives should make sure there is sufficient yin energy.

- Do not have water on the right side of the door: on the inside or the outside. This is said to give the man of the house a roaming eye.

- Do not have water in the bedroom as this causes loss.

- Beware of swimming pools. Large bodies of water can drown relationships, especially if they are located in the southwest.

- Put a bright light, five feet above the ground, in the southwest of the garden.

- If the kitchen is in the southwest then it is detrimental to love luck. However, if the stove is in the southwest of the kitchen it nullifies the bad effect because fire strengthens the earth element.

- It is okay to have different bed directions for each partner. Even separate bedrooms are okay if the gua directions are incompatible.

- On a date, sit facing your relationship direction.

- Sleep with your head toward your relationship direction.

SOLVING CAREER PROBLEMS

- Enhance the northern sector with water. Use wavy shapes, and blue or black colors in decoration.

- Support with metal, the color white, and round shapes.

- Avoid wood and plants, green colors, and rectangular shapes.

- Career luck is destroyed by the earth element, ocher colors, and square shapes in the north, so avoid those.

- Keep a turtle or tortoise in the north, either living or metal.

- Have a small fountain, aquarium, or pond in the north—as long as it is not behind the building.

- Avoid having plants in the north.

- Use your wealth direction at work. Sit facing this direction at your desk, at meetings, and when negotiating.

- Travel to work from your wealth direction.

- Use doors that face your wealth direction.

- Have the phone plugs coming from your wealth direction.

- Implement the tips on page 142 on how to maximize your mentor luck.

- Beware of poison arrows in the office.

- Do not sit directly under a ceiling fan.

- Be careful what you put on the desk. Beware of sharp objects pointing at you. Do not have images of wild animals facing you.

- Do not pile up files in front of you. Have them behind you or to the side. Behind, they form a mountain, which gives support.

- Apply the Lo Shu square to your desk: have a bright lamp in the south of your desk, put flowers in the east or south, and position computers and telephones in the west or northwest.

- Try to locate the desk in the corner opposite, and facing away from, the door. Then orient the desk in your wealth direction.

- Do not sit directly opposite someone.

- Have a solid wall or a screen behind.

- Have a picture of a mountain behind.

- Also have a representation of a turtle behind.

- Do not sit in a triangular-shaped room. If you have no choice then make it regular-shaped using mirrors and furniture, but do not sit facing a mirror.

- Avoid a room with a sloping ceiling. If there is no choice then sit under the high part and shine a light up at the lower part to combat it.

- Do not sit with your back to a window—or if you must, cover it with solid blinds. Though if there is a large building behind you it is okay to leave the blinds and windows open.

- Do not have an office at the end of a long corridor; a meandering path to your office or workstation is better.

- Use the Qian trigram (three unbroken lines) in decoration.

- Beware of bathrooms, beams, pillars, corners, and exposed shelves.

- An image of a dragon is good in the east or southeast of the office or table.

SOLVING HEALTH PROBLEMS

Health problems are the most difficult to solve. There are not so many tips in geomancy as for other problems.

- Use big wood, dark green colors, and rectangular shapes in the eastern sectors.

- Support this with water, black and blue colors, and wavy shapes.

- Avoid fire, excessive light, red, and triangular colors.

- Especially avoid metal objects, the color white, and round shapes.

- Put a representation of a green dragon in the east sector but not if this is in a bedroom. If this is the case, put the dragon image in the east of the garden.

- Use the health direction for sleeping. Remember you must always sleep with your head toward the auspicious direction—not your feet.

- Do not have a bathroom in the east because there is no cure for the ill luck this will cause.

- Protect yourself from poison arrows, especially next to your bed.

- Do not sleep between a bathroom and a window or door.

- Cure a missing corner in the east using the same methods explained in the section on wealth.

- Avoid sleeping in a bedroom that is afflicted by the Five Yellows that year.

- Do not have a spiral staircase in the eastern sector.

- Place three big plants in the east sector of the house or garden.

- According to the table of the trigrams in chapter 1, certain parts of the body will be negatively affected if the corresponding sectors are missing or afflicted. If you have particular health problems, check the relevant sectors. For instance, if you have problems with your eyes, check the southern sector of the land, the house, the living room, and the bedroom; remove the negative elements (water and earth) and increase the enhancing elements (fire and wood).

- From a Buddhist perspective, the cause of good health and long life is not killing, including all animals. Releasing them back into the wild and saving them from being killed is very good.

SOLVING CHILDREN'S PROBLEMS

If you are having trouble conceiving a child, or are having trouble—whether health, academic, or behavioral—with the ones you have, try these tips.

- Put small metal objects, the color white, and round shapes in the western sectors.

- Support the western sector with earth, ocher colors, square shapes.

- If the child is rebellious, change the bed direction to their relationships direction.

- Beware of poison arrows next to their beds and desks.

- Cure missing corners in the west.

- In the bathroom, do not have pictures of children.

- Do not have a bathroom in the west. If you do, hang a large six-rod wind chime there.

- Children's bedrooms should be more yang than yin. This is because they are growing and should be full of energy. So a television, stereo, and bright colors are all good.

- This does not mean that there should be total absence of yin energy. Arrange the lights so that there is some yin around the bed, or use yin colors for bedding.

- Avoid pictures of aggressive animals or symbols of war. Keep war toys stored away.

- The bed should always be in the Compass School development direction for children.

- Desks should also face the development direction.

- Avoid having a window or door behind the chair where the child studies.

- Avoid poison arrows, especially beams, corners of cupboards, exposed shelves, hooks, and nails.

- Do not have a tree growing too close to the bedroom window and blocking the light.

- Hang a crystal pendant in the northeast window to catch the morning light.

- Put a lamp with a glass shade in the northeast.

- Put a globe in the northwest for help from teachers and mentors.

- Put metal trophies in the west or northwest.

- Put wooden objects in the east and southeast for health and wealth.

- Put a picture of a turtle or tortoise, or a metal one, in the north. Remember there should be no water in the bedroom.

SOLVING KNOWLEDGE AND ACADEMIC PROBLEMS

- Activate the northeastern sectors with the small earth element; use crystals, square shapes and ocher colors.

- Support the northeast with the fire element: lights, red colors, triangle shapes.

- Avoid metal, the color white, and round shapes.

- Wood is destructive in the northeast. Do not have plants, wood, green colors, or rectangular shapes.

- Compensate for an external missing corner in the northeast with a high, bright light and a boulder.

- Face your development direction when studying.

- Sleep with your head toward your wealth or development direction.

- Avoid poison arrows.

- Use success symbols such as rosettes and trophies. Keep metal trophies in the west part of the room.

- Implement the tips from the section on mentor luck on the next page.

- When you take examinations, sit facing your wealth or development direction.

- Put a globe in the northwest of your study or bedroom.

SOLVING REPUTATION PROBLEMS

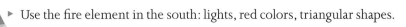 - Use the fire element in the south: lights, red colors, triangular shapes.

  - Support the sector with wooden objects and plants, green colors, and rectangular shapes.

- Avoid the earth element, ocher colors, and square shapes.

- Water, blue or black colors, and wavy shapes destroy reputation luck.

- Use the relationship or wealth directions when you are sleeping and sitting.

- Keep a tortoise in the north.

- Avoid having a bathroom in the south.

- Cure a missing corner in the south.

- Do not sit with your back to the Three Killings.

- Spiral staircases are negative in every sector, especially for reputation luck in the southern sector.

- Avoid poison arrows.

SOLVING PROBLEMS IN GETTING HELP FROM MENTORS

▶ Use the big metal element in the northwest. Hang a five-rod metal wind chime. Use the color white and round shapes.

▶ Support the sector with the earth element, square shapes, and ocher colors.

▶ Avoid water, wavy shapes, and blue and black colors.

▶ Fire is destructive so avoid excessive lighting, red colors, and triangular shapes.

▶ Sleep and sit in your relationship or wealth directions.

▶ Keep a tortoise in the north.

▶ Do not have a bathroom in the northwest. If you do, cure it with a six-rod wind chime.

▶ It is strongly recommended that you do not have the kitchen in the northwest.

▶ Avoid poison arrows.

▶ Have a picture of a mountain behind you at work and when studying.

▶ Keep a horseshoe-shaped magnet in the northwest, with the "U" shape upward, not downward. This should attract mentor luck.

▶ Use the Qian trigram (three unbroken lines) in decoration in your office, in the ceiling cornice and on the desk.

Afterword

I N HIS PUBLIC TALKS, His Holiness the Dalai Lama always exhorts his audience to be good-hearted people; he says, "My religion is kindness." All the major religious philosophies of the world promote wisdom, loving kindness, compassion, humility, patience, and peace as being among the most important human qualities to possess. These are the causes of true happiness—geomancy on its own is not sufficient.

As you enjoy the fruits of your own positive actions through the application of geomancy techniques, please remember to pass on your good fortune to others. In this way you will create further seeds of success and ensure your own and others' long-term benefit. Then wherever you go in the universe you will find happiness.

Acknowledgments

I AM INDEBTED to Lama Zopa Rinpoche for lighting the spark of my interest in geomancy and to Lillian Too for her encouragement and help. Also to Grand Master Yap Cheng Hai for fuelling my interest. I am also indebted to many friends who have encouraged me and made recommendations to others, especially Tony and Alison Steel, Greg Hitchen, Tara Melwani and her family, and Dr. Marla Tun. I am especially grateful to all my friends in France and Italy for encouraging me to write this book.

I want to thank all my friends at Sera Je Monastery for their support, especially Ven. Kunchock Dhondup for his inexhaustible patience, and Osel for all his kindness and for giving the title of this book.

Appendix: Gua Numbers for Birthdates near the Chinese New Year

Birth date	Animal	Gua Number	
		Male	Female
Feb 18, 1912 – Feb 5, 1913	Mouse	7	8
Feb 6, 1913 – Jan 25, 1914	Ox	6	9
Jan 26, 1914 – Feb 13, 1915	Tiger	5	1
Feb 14, 1915 – Feb 2, 1916	Rabbit	4	2
Feb 3, 1916 – Jan 22, 1917	Dragon	3	3
Jan 23, 1917 – Feb 10, 1918	Snake	2	4
Feb 11, 1918 – Jan 31, 1919	Horse	1	5
Feb 1, 1919 – Feb 19, 1920	Sheep	9	6
Feb 20, 1920 – Feb 7, 1921	Monkey	8	7
Feb 8, 1921 – Jan 27, 1922	Bird	7	8

Birth Date	Animal	Male	Female
Jan 28, 1922 – Feb 15, 1923	Dog	6	9
Feb 16, 1923 – Feb 4, 1924	Pig	5	1
Feb 5, 1924 – Jan 23, 1925	Mouse	4	2
Jan 24, 1925 – Feb 12, 1926	Ox	3	3
Feb 13, 1926 – Feb 1, 1927	Tiger	2	4
Feb 2, 1927 – Jan 22, 1928	Rabbit	1	5
Jan 23, 1928 – Feb 9, 1929	Dragon	9	6
Feb 10, 1929 – Jan 29, 1930	Snake	8	7
Jan 30, 1930 – Feb 16, 1931	Horse	7	8
Feb 17, 1931 – Feb 5, 1932	Sheep	6	9
Feb 6, 1932 – Jan 25, 1933	Monkey	5	1
Jan 26, 1933 – Feb 13, 1934	Bird	4	2
Feb 14, 1934 – Feb 3, 1935	Dog	3	3
Feb 4, 1935 – Jan 23, 1936	Pig	2	4
Jan 24, 1936 – Feb 10, 1937	Mouse	1	5
Feb 11, 1937 – Jan 30, 1938	Ox	9	6
Jan 31, 1938 – Feb 18, 1939	Tiger	8	7
Feb 19, 1939 – Feb 7, 1940	Rabbit	7	8
Feb 8, 1940 – Jan 26, 1941	Dragon	6	9
Jan 27, 1941 – Feb 14, 1942	Snake	5	1

Birth Date	Animal	Male	Female
Feb 15, 1942 – Feb 4, 1943	Horse	4	2
Feb 5, 1943 – Jan 24, 1944	Sheep	3	3
Jan 25, 1944 – Feb 12, 1945	Monkey	2	4
Feb 13, 1945 – Feb 1, 1946	Bird	1	5
Feb 2, 1946 – Jan 21, 1947	Dog	9	6
Jan 22, 1947 – Feb 9, 1948	Pig	8	7
Feb 10, 1948 – Jan 28, 1949	Mouse	7	8
Jan 29, 1949 – Feb 16, 1950	Ox	6	9
Feb 17, 1950 – Feb 5, 1951	Tiger	5	1
Feb 6, 1951 – Jan 26, 1952	Rabbit	4	2
Jan 27, 1952 – Feb 13, 1953	Dragon	3	3
Feb 14, 1953 – Feb 2, 1954	Snake	2	4
Feb 3, 1954 – Jan 23, 1955	Horse	1	5
Jan 24, 1955 – Feb 11, 1956	Sheep	9	6
Feb 12, 1956 – Jan 30, 1957	Monkey	8	7
Jan 31, 1957 – Feb 17, 1958	Bird	7	8
Feb 18, 1958 – Feb 7, 1959	Dog	6	9
Feb 8, 1959 – Jan 27, 1960	Pig	5	1
Jan 28, 1960 – Feb 14, 1961	Mouse	4	2
Feb 15, 1961 – Feb 4, 1962	Ox	3	3

Birth Date	Animal	Male	Female
Feb 5, 1962 – Jan 24, 1963	Tiger	2	4
Jan 25, 1963 – Feb 12, 1964	Rabbit	1	5
Feb 13, 1964 – Feb 1, 1965	Dragon	9	6
Feb 2, 1965 – Jan 20, 1966	Snake	8	7
Jan 21, 1966 – Feb 8, 1967	Horse	7	8
Feb 9, 1967 – Jan 29, 1968	Sheep	6	9
Jan 30, 1968 – Feb 16, 1969	Monkey	5	1
Feb 17, 1969 – Feb 5, 1970	Bird	4	2
Feb 6, 1970 – Jan 26, 1971	Dog	3	3
Jan 27, 1971 – Feb 14, 1972	Pig	2	4
Feb 15, 1972 – Feb 2, 1973	Mouse	1	5
Feb 3, 1973 – Jan 22, 1974	Ox	9	6
Jan 23, 1974 – Feb 10, 1975	Tiger	8	7
Feb 11, 1975 – Jan 30, 1976	Rabbit	7	8
Jan 31, 1976 – Feb 17, 1977	Dragon	6	9
Feb 18, 1977 – Feb 6, 1978	Snake	5	1
Feb 7, 1978 – Jan 27, 1979	Horse	4	2
Jan 28, 1979 – Feb 15, 1980	Sheep	3	3
Feb 16, 1980 – Feb 4, 1981	Monkey	2	4
Feb 5, 1981 – Jan 24, 1982	Bird	1	5
Jan 25, 1982 – Feb 12, 1983	Dog	9	6

Birth Date	Animal	Male	Female
Feb 13, 1983 – Feb 1, 1984	Pig	8	7
Feb 2, 1984 – Feb 19, 1985	Mouse	7	8
Feb 20, 1985 – Feb 8, 1986	Ox	6	9
Feb 9, 1986 – Jan 28, 1987	Tiger	5	1
Jan 29, 1987 – Feb 16, 1988	Rabbit	4	2
Feb 17, 1988 – Feb 5, 1989	Dragon	3	3
Feb 6, 1989 – Jan 26, 1990	Snake	2	4
Jan 27, 1990 – Feb 14, 1991	Horse	1	5
Feb 15, 1991 – Feb 3, 1992	Sheep	9	6
Feb 4, 1992 – Jan 22, 1993	Monkey	8	7
Jan 23, 1993 – Feb 9, 1994	Bird	7	8
Feb 10, 1994 – Jan 30, 1995	Dog	6	9
Jan 31, 1995 – Feb 18, 1996	Pig	5	1
Feb 19, 1996 – Feb 6, 1997	Mouse	4	2
Feb 7, 1997 – Jan 27, 1998	Ox	3	3
Jan 28, 1998 – Feb 15, 1999	Tiger	2	4
Feb 16, 1999 – Feb 4, 2000	Rabbit	1	5
Feb 5, 2000 – Jan 23, 2001	Dragon	9	6
Jan 24, 2001 – Feb 11, 2001	Snake	8	7
Feb 12, 2002 – Jan 31, 2003	Horse	7	8
Feb 1, 2003 – Jan 21, 2004	Sheep	6	9

Birth Date	Animal	Male	Female
Jan 22, 2004 – Feb 8, 2005	Monkey	5	1
Feb 9, 2005 – Jan 28, 2006	Bird	4	2
Jan 29, 2006 – Feb 17, 2007	Dog	3	3
Feb 18, 2007 – Feb 6, 2008	Pig	2	4
Feb 7, 2008 – Jan 25, 2009	Mouse	1	5
Jan 26, 2009 – Feb 13, 2010	Ox	9	6
Feb14, 2010 – Feb 2, 2011	Tiger	8	7
Feb 3, 2011 – Jan 22, 2012	Rabbit	7	8
Jan 23, 2012 – Feb 9, 2013	Dragon	6	9
Feb 10, 2013 – Jan 30, 2014	Snake	5	1
Jan 31, 2014 – Feb 18, 2015	Horse	4	2
Feb 19, 2015 – Feb 7, 2016	Sheep	3	3
Feb 8, 2016 – Jan 27, 2017	Monkey	2	4
Jan 28, 2017 – Feb 15, 2018	Bird	1	5
Feb 16, 2018 – Feb 4, 2019	Dog	9	6
Feb 5, 2019 – Jan 24, 2020	Pig	8	7
Jan 25, 2020 – Feb 11, 2021	Mouse	7	8
Feb 12, 2021 – Jan 31, 2022	Ox	6	9
Feb 1, 2022 – Jan 21, 2023	Tiger	5	1
Jan 22, 2023 – Feb 9, 2024	Rabbit	4	2

About the Author

VEN. JAMPA LUDRUP started his working career as a science teacher and in 1979 moved into the information technology industry. He spent fifteen years in computer education and writing before undertaking a complete change of lifestyle when he became a Buddhist monk in the Tibetan tradition.

In 1996 Ven. Jampa was an attendant to Ven. Lama Zopa Rinpoche during his tour of Nepal, India, Singapore, and Malaysia. At this time Lama Zopa made his first contact with feng shui Grand Master Yap Cheng Hai and world-renowned expert and prolific author Lillian Too.

With Lama Zopa's encouragement, Ven. Jampa made a study of their system of feng shui, and after personal experiment he started to give advice and consultations.

From 1998 he has been resident at Sera Je Monastic University in South India, where he has studied Buddhism as well as serving as English language studies tutor to Ven. Lama Osel Rinpoche from 1998 to 2003.

Since 2003 he has been much in demand, and has given feng shui courses and consultancy to many businesses, institutions, and individuals all across the globe. In 2012 he made his tenth world tour.

Contact him at www.jlgeomancy.com.

About Wisdom Publications

WISDOM PUBLICATIONS is dedicated to offering works relating to and inspired by Buddhist traditions.

To learn more about us or to explore our other books, please visit our website at www.wisdompubs.org.

You can subscribe to our e-newsletter or request our print catalog online, or by writing to:

Wisdom Publications
199 Elm Street
Somerville, Massachusetts 02144 USA

You can also contact us at 617-776-7416, or info@wisdompubs.org.

Wisdom is a nonprofit, charitable 501 (c)(3) organization, and donations in support of our mission are tax deductible.

Wisdom Publications is affiliated with the Foundation for the Preservation of the Mahayana Tradition (FPMT).